The

The True Story of Serial Killer Peter Manuel

by

C.L. Swinney

The Beast of Birkenshaw

The True Story of Serial Killer Peter Manuel

by

C.L. Swinney

Copyrighted

RJ Parker Publishing, Inc.

03.2016

ISBN-13: 978-1530109388
ISBN-10: 1530109388

http://RJParkerPublishing.com/

Published in the United States of America

,

Copyrights

"You can have various aspects to a psychopathic personality; indifference to people's feelings, manipulating, lying... What is really fascinating about Manuel [Peter Manuel] is he ticks every box."
Dr. Richard Goldberg, Reader in Law, Aberdeen University

"The foulest beast on earth... A reptile in disguise, and rat of Birkenshaw."
From a poem written by Peter Manuel describing himself

"A man may be very bad without being mad."
Lord Cameron talking about the mental state of Peter Manuel

"Turn up the radio, and I'll go quietly."
Peter Manuel's last words

Table of Contents

Thank you to my Publisher, editor, proof-readers, and cover artist for your support:

- - **Chris**

RJ Parker Publishing, Aeternum Designs (book cover), Bettye McKee (editor), and proof-readers:

Lorrie Suzanne Phillippe, Marlene Fabregas, Darlene Horn, Ron Steed, Katherine McCarthy, Robyn MacEachern, Lee Knieper Husemann, Kathi Garcia, Vicky Matson-Carruth, and Linda H. Bergeron

Prologue

East Kilbride, Glasgow, South Lanarkshire, United Kingdom, January 2, 1956

Golf course where Anne Kneilands was murdered by serial killer Peter Manuel.

Seventeen-year-old Anne Kneilands, a pretty girl from middle-class High Blantyre, had many friends. Close to adulthood with her entire life ahead of her, Anne met life head on with great passion. That is until tragedy, in this case a chance encounter with a serial killer, struck swiftly and altered the young girl's life.

On January 2, 1956, around 2 p.m., Anne began to get ready for a night out dancing with her boyfriend...a night they'd been talking about for weeks. The plan included venturing to nearby Glasgow, to mingle and hang out, then dance the night away. By all accounts, every one of the kids wanted to celebrate the New Year by dancing.

Anne, like most teenage girls, must have gone round and round laying out dresses, hoping one would pop out for the evening. During the process, she received a call from her boyfriend. He explained he was suffering a terrible hangover from the Hogmanay (the night before) and, although he felt bad for doing so, he had to cancel their plan to visit Glasgow. Anne did not take the news well and she allowed frustration and sadness to creep in. She needed to share her grief with her girlfriend, another teenager living close by in East Kilbride. I suppose most kids would have been bummed out for sure, and Anne would not have known visiting her friend would be her last night on Earth.

*****

A young and slight white man, completely capable and very interested in the joy killing might bring him, noticed Anne

Kneilands leave her home and walk in the direction of East Kilbride. Instantly, a rush of adrenaline coursed through his veins. He'd not yet killed anyone up to this point in his life, but the thought of doing so had entertained him his entire adult life (and even as a teenager). This man had been laying pipe near the girl's home for almost a month and had noticed her the first day on the job. Perverted thoughts danced in his distorted brain since that moment several times a day...it wasn't love, it was infatuation mixed with lust and desire.

The construction worker left his worksite and followed the girl until she arrived at another home in East Kilbride. He could not completely explain at the time what it was about the girl that made him tick, but he wanted her. His warped mind quickly developed a plan to grab Anne and sexually attack her. The original plan, according to the suspect several years later, never included killing Anne (although I find it difficult to trust a serial killer's recollection).

Several hours passed while the life-long criminal sat in his car staring at the front door where his prey had disappeared. The anticipation of his pending attack and the unthinkable acts speeding through his thoughts sent blood to his loins and made his mouth water. He was no longer a human, but a disgusting shell of a young child left unattended and alone with menacing and unmentionable ideas and desires pummeling his psyche constantly. He'd fallen too far to ever be saved.

*****

Anne stayed with her friend for several hours until late into the evening. After saying their goodbyes, she left bundled up in her jacket and began walking a little over a mile back to her home. She walked along the East Kilbride Golf Course, a path she'd taken for years. We can only speculate as to what Anne must have heard that caused her to flee into the snow-covered golf course. Nevertheless, a short white man, later identified as serial killer Peter Anthony Manuel, gave chase to Anne.

The thought of seeing Peter, a career criminal angry at the world, bearing down on her must have been utterly frightening. I've seen that look several times over the years while working homicide and other serious cases. No words exist to properly explain that specific look. Anne processed the threat and knew instantly that she was in real danger. She turned and ran as fast as she could. I imagine the fierceness in Peter's eyes would have sent anyone fleeing and praying they would survive.

Peter pursued Anne like a hungry lion chases a gazelle, hoping to have his way with her once he caught her. Being faster and fueled with adrenaline, he caught Anne quickly, knocked her down, and then jumped on top of her and used his weight to pin her to the ground.

Anne's instincts to survive kicked into overdrive as she violently scratched at her attacker and wrestled with him trying to break free from his grasp. Sadly, his weight and determination to hurt her proved too much. It's unclear if Anne screamed or pled for help, but based on the late hour and her location (a deserted golf course away from the roadway), her screams may not have been answered. Based on the fact she cut Peter's face and chest, clear signs of trying to survive, I believe she screamed and did everything she could trying to save herself.

Peter, in a homicidal fit of rage,

continued trying to get Anne's panties down while fending off her arms and hands. He then tried to rape her and suddenly developed a new plan-the girl must die. He used an iron bar (conflicting information suggests the bar was either nearby or Peter had brought it with him) to beat Anne to death.

The whole chaotic senseless attack and murder lasted roughly two minutes. Peter, with his face and upper chest area bleeding and covered in Anne's blood, pushed himself up from the cold hard ground, stopped to look at Anne's lifeless body, then turned to sprint back to his car. He got in, started the car, and drove away as though nothing had happened. Anne's murder at his hands marked the beginning of a terrible two years in United Kingdom history.

*****

The following morning, George Gribbon of Blantyre, walked his dog along the golf course and discovered Anne's body. He scampered to nearby Calderglen Farm and told Jimmy Barr, the farmer there, of his discovery. According to records, Mr. Barr phoned the police and brewed a cup of tea for himself and Mr. Gribbon hoping the drink would calm their nerves.

Police responded to the scene, as did world renowned photographer Harry Benson. Mr. Benson allegedly heard one of the officers on scene state, "This is the work of Peter Manuel." This statement was never verified during my research, and it's unclear what about the scene would prompt an officer to immediately assume Peter Manuel was the killer, but if it was true, the instincts of the officer should have been listened to.

Police did not immediately identify the deceased as Anne Kneilands. However, they later learned of the victim's identity and much more about her life. Anne lived with two brothers and three sisters at the old Calderwood Castle Stables, an area near where Calderside Grove and Calderwood Gardens are today.

Police discovered early on in the investigation that Anne's date for the dance, a subject named "A. Murnin" (according to available police records), failed to meet Anne at the bus stop located in Capelrig, Maxwellton. They were supposed to take the bus from there to Glasgow. Police did not know at that time that the boy was home fast asleep trying to recover from the night before.

Young Mr. A. Murnin was located and questioned at his home. Police determined Mr. A. Murnin had nothing to do with Anne's murder. Admittedly, much of what is known of Mr. Murnin has been expunged and made unavailable, most likely since he was a juvenile and was ruled out for having any involvement in Anne's murder. The emotion he would have felt when he realized what had happened to Anne, and how his change in plans contributed to her death, would weigh on the youngster for some time.

A record check with local bus routes indicated that Anne boarded the "189 SMT" bus to go visit a friend, trying to forget that she'd been stood up by her boyfriend. She did not have much money, and a local person said she saw Anne near the Willow Tearoom in East Kilbride Village late into the evening.

Investigators also made the gruesome discovery that Anne's skull had been broken in several locations. Her boot prints as well as the attacker's shoe prints were used to confirm that Anne ran some distance before being caught from behind. Unfortunately, since it was dark, she did not see a barbed-wire fence and ran into the fence trying to escape. She managed to free herself and kept running, but she had some cuts as a result of the barbed wire.

One of the inspectors noticed that Anne's underwear and one of her stockings had been ripped off, but there was no evidence of sexual assault (a lack of semen, bruising, swelling, or blood). Several of Anne's possessions were found spread around and near her corpse, almost as though the killer had staged the items. Police could not tell if the staging was meant to trick them into believing something else had happened at the scene. In addition, they did not originally have any inclination that a serial killer had killed Anne. Since it was Peter's first known murder, the mention of a serial killer would not have been discussed.

The following day, investigators learned the identity of the young girl was that of Anne Kneilands. They learned she worked as a machinist and was well-liked in the community. None of the people involved in the case could even dream of a reason that someone would kill her so brutally.

Anne's parents reported her missing the day after police located her body. When they learned of her fate, unimaginable grief took over because as they retraced their steps the night before, they realized they must have driven by their daughter's body not knowing she'd been murdered.

Police traced a route they figured the killer would have used to leave the horrific scene hoping to find evidence along the path that would give them a lead. They felt the killer used Morrishall Road north to either the Blackbraes Road or Old Peddlars Way, both on the Long Calderwood Ridge. The killer then likely used Stoneymeadow Road and went over Generals' Bridge to Blantyre. Nothing pertinent to the case was found along this path, however.

Anne's underwear and a piece of iron thought to be the murder weapon were later found in the river (a point discussed in greater detail further along in this book).

East Kilbride New Town continued to grow as a town after Anne's murder, but where she'd been found on that night was not built upon. A mature oak tree is surrounded by cobblestones adjacent to High Common Road, in St Leonard's, marking the location where Anne met serial killer Peter Manuel.

None of the people on the case could recall seeing such destruction as they'd witnessed at the crime scene. The fact the victim was a female and a teenager left an extremely bitter taste in the investigating team's mouths. As with all of their cases, but even more so for this one, the team determined they would not rest until their victim's killer was caught.

News of the horrific murder - of a teenaged girl no less - rocked the town. The nature of the crime and the young age of the victim hit parents, especially those with teenagers (and girls), extremely hard. A negative buzz spread throughout the community.

Based on the perceived sexual assault (it would later be determined Anne was not sexually assaulted) to the victim, local Lanarkshire Police officers began compiling a list of sexual offenders known to live or visit the area where the crime was committed. The list of names police complied was small.

One of the officers recognized one of the names from the list, that of Peter Thomas Anthony Manuel. The officer had previous contacts with Peter and he described him as a prolific burglar and a "creep."

A short inquiry revealed that Peter Manuel had been living and working in the area of Anne's murder. Investigators discovered that Peter worked for the gas board - his job was to place pipes into the ground meant for the growing area of East Kilbride New Town. Police quickly noticed that the gas board had a job site close to where Anne resided.

However, when police originally went to Peter's parents' home to speak to him, they were unable to locate him. Police then called his employer, the gas board. The employer advised them that Peter had not shown up to work, and he had not been seen or heard from for two days. The employer mentioned that Peter was a hard worker and it was not like him to miss work.

Police grew wary that a possible suspect (Peter Manuel) in the murder of Anne Kneilands may have skipped town. Multiple law enforcement members drove around the streets looking for Peter Manuel. At the same time, members of the public demanded answers and wanted to know why the killer had not been caught yet. Beyond speculation about Peter's possible involvement in the case, police had no other leads or evidence that they could release in an effort to calm the community.

Remember that in 1956, gathering and using DNA from crime scenes was not commonplace. Had the police done so, they might have gathered Peter's skin from Anne's fingernails from when she scratched and clawed at him during the attack. Tension began to climb in the community, forcing the Lanarkshire officers and detectives to broaden their search for Peter. Essentially, someone needed to be apprehended, questioned, and sent to prison for what they'd done to young Anne Kneilands. The community would not rest until justice was served and they could rest easier knowing a killer was no longer free to kill again.

On January 4th, Peter Manuel returned to work. His boss noticed Peter's face had scratches on it and remembered how the police were looking for him the day prior. Peter's boss was also aware of the murder of

Anne and the bits and pieces of the case slowly leaking out in the news. Discreetly, Peter's boss called the Lanarkshire detectives and told them that Peter had returned to work. Although his boss had heard rumblings of Peter being a shady character, he still did not suspect him of being capable of brutally killing an innocent teenaged girl.

Lanarkshire investigators and several beat officers were sent to speak to Peter. Once they arrived, and Peter noticed them, he cracked a wry smile. None of them knew what to think about the nonchalant glare on Peter's face, but more than one detective recalled that the way he looked at them concerned them greatly. They could not know just how devious and manipulative Peter had become. Peter willingly went with the police to the station to discuss whether he had any information (or an alibi) for his whereabouts when Anne Kneilands had been murdered.

While at the police station, detectives noticed scratches on Peter's face and chest. He calmly stated he obtained the scratches while rough-housing with his parents' dog. The investigators noted how calm Peter presented himself while being questioned, but some at the station still felt he was lying.

A criminal record check confirmed that Peter was already a life-long criminal, but was he also a cold-blooded killer?

When asked about his whereabouts on the evening of January 2nd, Peter told them he was with his father, Samuel, and added they were both home throughout the entire evening. Investigators were now obligated to verify Peter's claim. As Peter spoke to the detectives, he presented as being somewhat cocky and slightly arrogant - as though he enjoyed playing with the detectives. Although we later learn Peter Manuel never finished high school, it's believed his IQ was quite high. Peter also recalled later (while in prison) that he was "playing with the cops in the beginning."

Detectives pushed much harder with Peter. They asked him why he didn't return to work and where he was between January 2nd and January 4th. Again, he could (or would) not provide a detailed description of his whereabouts or activity during the time Anne was killed, nor did he have an answer as to why he didn't return to work for a few days. He spoke in circles, but some of what he said made sense. Eventually, faced with the information in front of them and the statement provided by Peter, some of the investigators openly considered he might be telling the truth and had nothing to do with Anne's murder. Nevertheless, police kept him at the station while investigators tried to locate his father to verify his alibi.

Hours later, Samuel Manuel was located and provided a similar statement as Peter - they were together at their home the entire evening of January 2nd. Without further evidence or an incriminating statement, Peter could not be held for the murder of Anne Kneilands. It was clear Peter Manuel was a disturbing man, but they had nothing linking him to the crime scene and he had presented a valid alibi. Therefore, Peter Manuel was begrudgingly let go. Tragically, his release would lead to several serial murders.

The fact Peter Manuel continued to kill *after* being released doesn't fall on the Lanarkshire Police. I've investigated numerous homicide cases over my career, and although they've all been unique, one thing remains the same. If I don't have the evidence and facts to support probable cause to arrest someone for murder (or any other crime), I have to let them go. Probable cause in America has the same meaning and power as it does in the United Kingdom. The officers knew Peter Manuel was a highly disturbed individual and felt he was capable of murder, and some felt he'd killed Anne, but they needed more to arrest him for murder.

Many of these cases don't really begin until presented in court (after a suspect is arrested). If you don't have the quality evidence to convince a judge and jury that your criminal is guilty, you're wasting everyone's time. In addition, being focused on one suspect based on a "hunch" can be dangerous, especially if you're wrong. The real killer may go free and continue to kill while you try to convince others that your hunch is right. In the case of Peter Manuel, he was allowed to leave the police station and resume his dangerous and filthy life. Within eight months of being released after being questioned about Anne's murder, Peter began plotting to kill again. This time, there'd be numerous victims at one crime scene, and the citizens of Burnside, Glasgow, would not be the same.

A Serial Killer is Born

New York City, New York, March 13, 1927

A male child was born to Samuel and Bridget Manuel in Manhattan, New York, United States. The Scottish immigrant parents named their second son Peter Thomas Anthony Manuel. His older brother, James Manuel, was born in 1925. Mr. and Mrs. Manuel had moved to the United States looking for the American dream, but shortly after Peter was born, the U.S. economy was struck by the Great Depression, and the family fell on difficult financial times.

In 1932, Samuel Manuel became significantly ill, forcing his wife to spend almost all of her time taking care of him. Providing him care left little time to find ways to put food on the table. With very little money and Mr. Manuel being sick, Bridget convinced him to move the family back to Motherwell (Lanarkshire), Scotland.

Mr. and Mrs. Manuel knew the move would be difficult, but many other family members would be closer by and could help take care of a struggling Samuel Manuel. Sam announced the family would move shortly thereafter, and Lanarkshire became the home where Peter Manuel would be raised. Unfortunately, Peter, five years old at the time, immediately began having issues growing up in a new country.

Children can be quite mean sometimes. In Peter's case, his "heavy" American accent brought on a lot of negative attention. He was bullied constantly while attending Our Lady of Good Aid School in Motherwell. Neighborhood children also teased him daily about his accent as well as for being shorter than everyone else.

His father remained sick and his mother was completely overwhelmed. Within two years, in 1934, his mother gave birth to Teresa Manuel, who required what little attention his parents had left. Peter was basically left to fend for himself, and he had a difficult time because of it.

Bored, angry, and desperate, Peter eventually committed his first crime at the age of nine. It was the first of hundreds of crimes that would follow.

Strangely, even while committing crimes, Peter still attended school. Records indicate he was enrolled at the School of S. S. Elisabeth and Helen in Coventry at the time he committed his first crime, that of breaking into a school building, occurred. The bullying continued and it obviously weighed heavy on Peter's mind. For a time, Peter found a way to rise above the childhood trauma and won a scholarship to King Henry VIII Grammar School. Just as it appeared Peter was making progress and the novelty of his accent began to slowly wear off, Peter was forced to make a choice - commit more crimes (which appealed to him) or obey his parents, teachers, and law enforcement (which he did not want to do). He chose a life of crime.

After being caught for breaking and entering for a second time, he was sent to St. Gilbert's Approved School. Peter struggled there for six months and later ran away from the school. From this point on, Peter would enter and leave five more schools in a period of three years. It was clear Peter had other things on his mind, and school was not in his life plans. He was bored and looking for a challenge.

Once he turned ten years old, most of the Lanarkshire Police department knew him as a "bad kid" who stole a lot. His parents said they couldn't manage him, and Peter's behavior spiraled out of control. As such, he was labeled as having "issues," both mentally and behaviorally, and the task of figuring out what to do with him began. Eventually, after several months of failed attempts to correct his behavior, Peter was officially placed on probation.

Peter's probation officer would remark many years later that Peter "had the worst criminal" record he'd ever seen. It's difficult to think of children as criminals, but left unattended and without structure, children can be every bit as cunning and evil as any adult. We see examples of terrible crimes committed by children around the globe.

In 1938, the Manuel family moved to Coventry, England. The change in address did nothing to change Peter's poor behavior. No one took the time to address his behavior. He later lamented that he felt no one cared about him or what he did (except his parents because they understood him). He was a lost child growing more angry and resentful with each day that passed. His American accent and short stature made him an easy target for the bullies wherever he went. He wasn't much of a fighter at the time, but he acted out by committing crimes.

In 1939, at the age of twelve, Peter was arrested for breaking and entering, shoplifting, and larceny. Police caught him at the scene and held him in custody for the juvenile trial. He was found guilty of the crimes. Peter readily admitted that he enjoyed breaking into homes and he showed no remorse for the illegal activity he committed.

Since he was already known to law enforcement and clearly going down the wrong path, the judge ordered he be placed on supervised probation, hoping the extra attention of a probation officer would curtail his wrongdoings. Sadly, the order did nothing to change him. In fact, he would later say he only grew angrier as a result of having to deal with a probation officer on top of all the complaints he received from his parents and family. Peter had no regard for other people, their property, or homes. No one cared about him, so why would he care about anyone else?

In January of 1942, while on probation, Peter broke into his teacher's home while his wife, Barbara, was home. According to Peter, his teacher had embarrassed him in class. Peter decided he'd embarrass his teacher and break into his home. Unfortunately, his teacher was not home when Peter broke in. Peter later said he "snapped," saw a candle holder on the living room table, grabbed it, and proceeded to beat Barbara, whom he'd found asleep in her bed when he was searching for items to steal. He did not kill her, but she was seriously injured. Peter, after realizing what he'd just done, fled the home and knew he was in big trouble. He found a hiding spot at his school's nativity scene and remained there for several hours.

Peter's teacher returned home and found his wife injured. He called the police and then an ambulance. During the discussion between the teacher and his wife of what happened, Peter's teacher was able to identify Peter as the attacker. The police began looking for Peter and were quite motivated to find him. They were concerned because this assault was the first time he'd hurt someone. They knew him to be a property thief, not someone to attack people. The fact he beat a woman with a candle holder demonstrated his activity had further deteriorated and police now needed to add violent acts to his already long criminal history. Peter, once a property crime specialist, had added violent behavior to his actions.

The police found Peter a short time later and arrested him for breaking and entering and for assaulting his teacher's wife.

However, while this case was processed and heard in a court of law, Peter was not in custody. The fact he was released was a matter of protocol back then, but this turned out to be a fatal mistake in the life of Peter Manuel.

Since the age of seven, he'd been committing crime, and now he'd escalated to violence against a person. He was on probation at the time he attacked Barbara. Nevertheless, he was free and didn't waste any time committing more crimes. After committing so many crimes and rarely having any sort of repercussion for doing them, Peter was not deterred from continuing down his dangerous life path. Admittedly, he enjoyed causing havoc and craved attention.

Between January and June, while still on probation and currently having another case being heard in juvenile court, Peter committed at least three known breaking and entering crimes. He would later say the rush of breaking into homes aroused him, and he found each place he selected to steal from to be a challenge. He lamented that no home was safe when he was around.

In June of 1942, police arrested Peter and his case was referred to the Southport Juvenile Court system. He remained in custody for a few days, but the court, hoping to keep Peter out of the judicial system and trying to let him have time to be with his family, again let him go. The court ordered he remain on probation and requested his probation officer keep close tabs on him. Yet again, this move did not change the fact that he was out of custody and free to do whatever he felt like doing.

No one took the time to actually talk to Peter, try to figure what was causing all of his anger. The probation officer was already over-worked and had numerous children on his case load. As it is today, a probation officer can never keep up with all of the clients on their case load. I was once a juvenile probation officer. I had seventy kids on my case load. I was able to see a few, but with so many kids to manage, I spent most of my time dealing with the ones who'd keep getting arrested. It's a thankless job, and with a juvenile, you have very little tools or leverage to get them to follow the rules or laws. Most of the kids on probation know this and make the probation officer's life miserable.

Peter Manuel's egregious criminal activity continued. He enjoyed what he was doing; it moved him emotionally, and he would steal items, mostly money, to buy things he wanted. His parents were too busy to notice their son spiraling out of control.

In March of 1943, after a string of seven more breaking and entering cases against him, Peter landed in the Market Weighton court system. He remained in custody this time as everyone (his parents, his probation officer, the local police officers, and the courts) had grown tired of him. The judge, taking into account the crimes Peter committed and his attitude of not caring about the people he hurt or his destructive pattern, ordered Peter to be committed to a borstal (prison for juveniles) for two years. The amount of time he was sentenced to was unprecedented for the time period, but well deserved.

While at the Rochester Borstal Institution, Peter would become even more jaded. His accent (although he had a slight American accent now after living in the UK for so long) and stature made him the butt of many jokes. The first day he was at the borstal, he wound up fighting a boy slightly larger than him. Fueled by rage, Peter beat the bully soundly, and the remaining kids left him alone...for the time being.

Peter did not have anyone to talk to while at the borstal, no way to address his inner demons, and like most prison systems, only learned how to better commit crimes while there. He did not change his mind about reckless or illegal activity and did not get the attention (psychological evaluation and game plan to correct his behavior) that he needed.

Not only was the borstal itself struggling based on the fact more emotional and unstable criminal children were being ordered there more commonly, but the system was not designed to identify or correct the behavior these kids displayed. A rather interesting bit of trivia pertaining to the case of Peter Manuel is the fact that the Rochester Borstal Institution was located in Rochester, within Kent, England.

As many of you know, World War II began in 1939 and waged on until 1945. Besides London, Kent was the most heavily targeted area for German Luftwaffe bombers.

Kent's towns were bombed throughout World War II, resulting in heavy casualties (even though raid sirens would ring and people would go underground). For a large percentage of the war, the Germans had complete control of the Channel, allowing them to bomb the Kent coast at will.

In June of 1944, the Germans sent close to 1,500 "Doodlebug" bombs around the county of Kent. A Doodlebug bomb was a pulsejet-guided cruise missile the Germans used quite often during the war. Gunners, Balloon Handlers, and the RAF struggled to hold and defend the frontline.

During one specific attack, Peter Manuel and many other juveniles at the borstal were injured from German bombing. Reports indicate that a piece of steel sent flying through the air after a bomb hit a nearby building struck Peter in the head and knocked him unconscious. Some reported that Peter was nowhere near the borstal during the air raid, but most of what I've read indicates he was there. Medical records also indicate that Peter received medical attention for the injury and was "blank minded" for several days. Based on the information available for this incident, it's likely Peter suffered a concussion as a result of the steel slamming him in the head. He was lucky to survive the German attack, but it's unclear what or if the head injury played a role in him becoming a serial killer.

As the war continued, Peter remained at the borstal under court order. Records show that he got in less trouble after he was injured during the bombing. However, the environment at the borstal, far from ideal, would impact how he behaved and what things he chose to find important.

In June of 1944, at the age of seventeen, Peter and several of the juveniles in the borstal got jobs working with a local electrician. The owner of the electrical company was intent on rebuilding Kent after the bombings. The contractor paid them well, but Peter and his friends did not receive proper training. The fact of the matter was there was too much work to be done to stop and train anyone about the dangers of working with electricity.

While on a job site, a fellow borstal inmate caused himself, Peter, and two other workers to get a significant electric shock. The electricity flowed through Peter's body - he lost consciousness and was burned badly on his arms. The boy who caused the accident and two others (one report stated three co-workers/borstal inmates) died as a result of the injuries they received. Peter was treated and survived the accident; however, he reported having significant memory loss issues afterwards and for several years to follow. He'd cheated death while being bombed and once again when being shocked.

In March of 1945, Peter was released from the Rochester Borstal Institution and found himself back into the community. He had no job, no income, nowhere to live, and had to decide once again, commit crime or struggle to survive? He eventually decided to move back in with his parents, but their relationship was obviously turbulent at best. They were happy to see him and loved him, but he'd been getting into trouble so long that they had no idea what to expect from him. Likewise, they were quite aware they would have no chance of controlling his behavior.

For the first few months after being released, Peter did odd jobs and spent time trying to make himself better (although his definition of "better" would vary greatly from yours or mine). It's unclear why, but for almost a full year, Peter apparently did not commit a crime and had no contact with local law enforcement.

Many believe (although Peter never confirmed this) that he was somewhat stable because he'd found a girlfriend. Based on my experience, it's more likely that Peter was in fact committing crime, but he was not getting caught while doing so. Jails, prisons, and borstals rarely teach people how to become contributing members of society. In fact, most of the people incarcerated in these situations re-offend and spend most of their time trying to figure out a way to commit more crime and not get caught.

On February 17, 1946, Peter (now an adult) entered a stranger's locked home and stole a watch from the homeowner. The victim saw Peter leaving the home when he returned from an errand and committed to memory Peter's physical description. The victim contacted the police, they responded to his home, and within minutes the officer on scene believed the suspect was Peter Manuel. The officer who'd responded wrote the initial breaking and entering report, found two of his police partners, and they spent a few hours looking for Peter.

Later in the day, an officer found Peter,

contacted him, and noticed Peter was wearing the watch that the victim reported as stolen a few hours prior. Naturally, Peter was arrested for breaking and entering and for being in possession of stolen property. He was, for the first time in his life, booked into an adult jail.

He would not be released from jail as a result of his arrest on the 17th for being in possession of a stolen watch until February 21, 1946, after a friend posted bail for him. Peter later admitted that the police had no idea what he'd been doing, what he was capable of, and what he'd been planning to do. Most of the local police knew him to be a prolific residential burglar, but Peter was about to graduate to being a full-fledged violent criminal.

At this point in his life, taking into account his childhood and all the crime he'd committed, considering he had no one in his family capable of policing him, and the fact he felt no one respected him, Peter made a decision in his mind to begin taking whatever it was he felt others owed him - even if that meant someone else's life.

While out on bail for the case

mentioned above, Peter spent time in the area of Mt. Vernon, Glasgow. He had no job, no income, and no means to provide for himself legally. As he reflected on his current pitiful state and the fact he was hungry and angry, an idea popped in his head to make things better for himself - at someone else's expense.

On March 3, 1946, a mother passed by Peter with her three-year-old child in tow. Peter, without provocation, jumped toward the woman and knocked her to the ground. With the woman's child watching, Peter repeatedly kicked her as she lay there screaming for help. He then jumped on top of her and punched her with his fists. Peter later admitted that the rush from the attack, and the fact that he was in complete control, aroused him. He did not, however, rape the victim or hurt her child. After gathering himself, Peter fled the area on foot, knowing police would be called soon. The incident, although terrifically violent and something no one should ever have to experience, lasted less than two minutes.

The victim and her sobbing child were spotted by a passerby who called the police. Obviously, the victim was shaken up. Her child was distraught after watching her mother get assaulted. Her wounds required medical attention, and she was woozy based on the repeated strikes to her head from the attacker.

Police responded to the area quickly. They summoned help for the victim and followed her and her child to the hospital.

Investigating such crimes is a touchy subject; you want to get information quickly about the attacker in an effort to catch the suspect as quickly as possible, but you don't want to do it in such a manner that it causes further strife for the victim. Investigators spent a considerable amount of time carefully questioning the victim, hoping to learn the identity of her attacker.

This case remained open allowing Peter to walk the streets, posing a serious risk to the community. The police were not aware that he was the woman's attacker. A short amount of time would pass before Peter Manuel struck again.

On March 7, 1946, a petite twenty-two-year-old nurse walked along Calder Road in Bellshill, North Lanarkshire, UK. She'd just finished a shift and was headed home to get some much-needed rest before being scheduled to return the following morning.

Peter drove by her and instantly decided he needed to speak to her. He pulled over well in front of her and parked along the curb. Peter exited his vehicle and waited about a half-block away for the nurse to get closer. Again, as he'd done in the first attack, Peter pounced on the woman as she got closer.

He pushed her to the ground and punched and elbowed her several times. The nurse tried to fend off Peter's attack by wiggling and screaming. However, Peter held his hand over her mouth with great force and she was unable to break free from his assault. Conflicting reports suggest Peter raped the victim; however, he was never charged with rape (when he was apprehended as a serial killer) in this attack, and no written verification exists (such as a police report) that would indicate Peter sexually assaulted the nurse. She was a victim, nevertheless, but she escaped certain death.

This second attack was approximately seven miles from where Peter attacked the mother with her child. Police responded to the area and worked hard to identify the nurse's assailant. She was cooperative with police and had fared much better than the first victim. The nurse provided a decent description of her attacker and was fairly confident she could identify him if she saw him again. Although the attacks were somewhat close to each other, none of the local police had connected both attacks as being committed by the same person. This case was also left open while police searched for evidence and the attacker. Peter Manuel, growing more confident, daring, and seeking greater control, would wait less than a day to attack a third victim.

On March 8, 1946, a twenty-five-year-old female stood outside her broken-down vehicle flagging people down, hoping someone would stop to help her. Her sedan was parked on Ferry Road in the town of Bothwell, South Lanarkshire, UK.

Peter, growing more brazen and needing to feel the power and arousal from attacking a woman and dominating her, happened to drive by the young woman. He parked ahead of her and worked his way toward the woman and her vehicle. For some time, he just stood in the shadows and watched her. He developed a plan to get her away from the street. At some point, he could no longer control his urges, and he attacked her several yards from her car still close to the main road.

During the attack, Peter became enraged and full of lust. Instead of punching and kicking her, he used his weight to grab her hair and smash her head on the cold hard ground - he'd dragged her into some nearby bushes and manhandled her with ease, fueled by adrenaline. While the victim lay unconscious, he proceeded to pull her pants down and raped her. As he raped her, the victim regained consciousness and somehow managed to push him off of her.

Peter was likely puzzled as to how she'd been able to move him, but his lengthy experience in the criminal world sent his internal clock reeling. The attack had taken place in broad daylight, and although he'd moved the victim away from the roadway, he was sure someone saw or heard something. Peter considered killing the woman but (and no one is sure why), he did not kill her. Instead he ran to his vehicle and fled the area believing he was too intelligent and sophisticated to ever be apprehended by the police.

The victim was able to identify many of Peter's physical and facial characteristics, giving the police leads to chase down. A pattern was also detected by an investigator loosely linking the three attacks - all three victims were young women and the attacks occurred close to golf courses. All three victims described similar physical characteristics of their attacker, too. Therefore, police were convinced a serial attacker (and possibly serial rapist) had chosen Lanarkshire for his hunting ground.

Police worked through the night and were able to come up with a possible suspect, one Peter Manuel. They prepared a line-up of photographs (one being Peter Manuel) and showed them to the third victim. She easily and quickly identified Peter Manuel as the man who beat and raped her.

On March 9, 1946, police located and apprehended Peter in Glasgow. He was formally charged with the assault and rape of the third victim, but the court case would take a while to be adjudicated. In the meantime, police throughout Glasgow and

Lanarkshire worked breaking-and-entering cases in their towns in which Peter was also considered the primary suspect.

On March 21, 1946, a judge sentenced Peter to a year in prison after finding him guilty of fifteen residential burglaries in the community. At the age of nineteen, and already a seasoned veteran of the criminal justice system in the United Kingdom, Peter literally smirked at the sentence, and it clearly did nothing to convince him to stop his egregious behavior.

Peter was sent to HM Prison Peterhead to begin serving time. Even though he'd been sent to prison, the rape and assault case that occurred on March 8, 1946, did not go away and continued while he was in custody.

On June 26, 1946, Peter was brought back to the High Court of Judiciary in Glasgow to stand trial for the assault and rape case. This case required two months to be heard in court. The jury immediately returned with guilty verdicts against Peter. Before being sentenced in the case, several other jurisdictions had filed cases against him as well. Each case needed to be heard and adjudicated per the law.

UK officials taxied Peter to court hearings in Ely, Manchester, Cambridge, Coventry, Hull, South Port, Yorkshire, Beverly, and Market Whiton. He was charged with breaking and entering into homes, businesses, and shops. The process of filing a case, presenting the case, and the case coming to a conclusion required time, and since Peter was still in custody, every law enforcement agency rushed to build cases against him, hoping to keep him in custody for a long time.

Eventually, in November of 1946, Peter was sentenced to six years in prison for the assault and rape case (and over thirty burglaries). He'd been committing crimes since the age of twelve (at least crime that was documented and left a paper trail) and finally, at the age of twenty, he would serve significant time behind bars (and be unable to terrorize the community).

A Serial Killer is Coming

HM Prison Barlinnie, Glasgow, UK, February 1953.

In February of 1953, Peter Manuel was released from HM Prison Barlinnie in Glasgow, UK. Records indicate he had several fights while in custody and, following my conclusions stated previously, Peter likely learned much more about how to commit a crime and not get caught than what it takes to be a contributing member in society. In addition, nothing in the records suggests he received counseling or support services that would have been necessary to curtail his improper desires or help him make sound decisions.

The prison system as a whole, particularly in the mid-1950s, was ill-prepared to handle someone such as Peter Manuel. In fact, by his own admission, he'd later toy with prison staff and manipulate them to do things "just for the hell of it." He was quite intelligent and found his time behind bars amusing at times. Yet there were many other times where darkness and anger fueled Peter to attack other prisoners, landing him in solitary confinement.

Nevertheless, Peter had matured slightly compared to when he first went to prison, but he became more cunning. Prison in any country is a sink-or-swim thing; you either make do or get run over. Peter learned to survive while in custody, but he stated how elated he was to see sunlight outside prison walls. At the time of his release, he did not have a plan of what his first course of action would be.

However, one of his requirements upon release (part of the parole process) was to locate a job. He interviewed for several possible jobs in Glasgow and Lanarkshire and finally managed to secure work as a pipe layer and fitter with the Gas Board Company (North Gas Board). After securing employment, Peter found a place to stay (a room in a house with a large family near Glasgow). Within a few months, he purchased a small used sedan.

For a time, he assimilated back into society and plugged along doing what everyone else (law enforcement, prison officials, family) wanted him to do. Still, disruptive thoughts of women, especially having the opportunity to dominate them again, crept back into his mind, confusing his inner demons. An urge to harm women constantly nagged at him.

Peter met a woman named Anne O'Hara a few months after being released from prison. He did not tell her about his tumultuous past. They dated off and on for about six months and eventually got engaged. Many believe the engagement and relationship he had with Anne is what kept him from committing crime (at least while they were together). As with many relationships, the couple began to have trouble, mostly in the form of verbal arguments.

On or about April 19, 1955, Anne called off the engagement. She cited their differences in religious beliefs as the reason for the break-up. Outwardly, Peter attempted to save face and told people it was *his* idea to call off the wedding. Inside, however, Peter would later state he was devastated by Anne's decision and vowed to make women (in general, with no real targets outlined at this time) pay for what he viewed as Anne's betrayal.

Peter could not believe Anne called off the marriage. He suddenly realized he was not in control of things, and it caused him to emotionally explode. Everything he'd suppressed from his childhood - the rush of residential burglaries and arousal he obtained while attacking women and what he'd been exposed to while in prison - all surfaced at once. A monster within Peter had been awakened, one that was previously, although temporarily, dormant within him.

Later that day (the day of the final break-up), Peter went back to doing what he knew rather well - assaulting young women. In a fit of rage, he drove around town seething because Anne had left him and hurt him terribly. According to Peter, he was also very upset that he let her get away with calling off the engagement, another example of him losing control.

Peter saw a woman walking down the street, one who looked a lot like his ex-fiancée Anne, and decided she (the unknown woman) would pay for Anne's mistake of leaving him. Peter, far more aggressive than in the past, jumped out of his vehicle and held a knife to the woman's throat. The victim, later identified as Mary McLaughlan, was terrified, and Peter forced her into his car.

He drove them out of the area with the knife pressed against Mary's chest. Peter parked in a desolate area fully intending to rape Mary...he also planned to kill her. She saw an opening during the time Peter struggled with getting his pants down and used it to push away from him, open the door, and run for her life.

At this point, Peter was enraged and completely prepared to kill her. He'd let Anne get away and now he let another woman get away. His carelessness caused him to curse out loud. He did not pursue Mary and decided to leave the area.

It's unclear where Peter went or what his plan was after this failed attack. In fact, for a brief period (the last few months of 1955), Peter Manuel stayed off the radar of law enforcement and prison officials. To their knowledge and based on available records during this timeframe, Peter did not commit a crime or attack another woman. I often wonder what exactly he was up to during this time period, but given his past and what he later would do, I cannot believe Peter Manuel was living "a normal life." In fact, I believe he was harming young women but getting away with it.

The year of 1956 would begin in the United Kingdom full of promise and people hoping to fulfill New Year's resolutions. Tragically, on the second day of the New Year, Peter Manuel chose to take the last drastic step toward becoming the United Kingdom's most infamous serial killer. He maliciously hunted and killed Anne Kneilands.

The murder sparked a fury inside Peter that he could not contain, nor did he wish to. Over the course of the next two years, he'd murder eight more people and hold residents across the country afraid and captive in their own homes. The Beast of Birkenshaw tormented and did unbelievable things to his victims that still cause a stir when discussed.

The Watt family Murders

Vivienne Watt

Marion and William Watt. William was accused of killing his wife, but in fact, she was murdered by Peter Manuel.

Burnside, Glasgow, September 17, 1956

Burnside, a quiet residential area in Rutherglen (South Lanarkshire) was (and still is) a wonderful place to raise a family in the mid-1950s. The Watt family, consisting of husband William Watt, his wife Marion Watt, and their daughter Vivienne Watt (aged seventeen at the time) lived in a modest home off of Stonelaw Road. Mrs. Watt's sister, Margaret Brown, was visiting at the time.

At approximately 10:43 p.m., while Vivienne, Margaret, and Marion were asleep in the home, Peter Manuel quietly broke a window panel in the side door, reached inside, and unlocked the door. He was armed with a handgun and looking for a quick score - something he'd been doing his entire adult life.

The thought of people being home did not originally cross Peter's mind, but he was prepared for anything when he did these robberies. He did not know three people were home, or that the husband of the house, William, was away on a fishing trip in Ardrishaig, nearly ninety miles away.

Once inside, Peter rummaged through drawers and cabinets looking for items to grab. Anything that seemed valuable ended up filling his jacket and pant pockets.

While searching the home for items to steal, Peter stumbled upon Marion Watt, fast asleep in her bedroom. Without provocation or regard for human life, Peter removed his handgun, aimed it at her head, and squeezed the trigger twice, instantly killing Marion.

He quickly searched the rest of the home and located Vivienne and Margaret; both had been startled by the boom Peter's pistol had made, but did not leave their beds. They must have been completely terror-stricken as they processed the gunshots they'd heard and now before them stood a serial killer. With no remorse, and fueled by lust after killing Marion, Peter shot and killed Vivienne and Margaret.

Peter did not leave the bodies alone, especially Vivienne. He got into her bed, removed parts of her clothing, and sexually assaulted her. Once he was done, he left her corpse, gathered himself, and went about searching for more items to steal.

Satisfied no more valuables remained

and his appetite for death quenched, Peter Manuel left the Watt family home and slipped into darkness once again. He got into his vehicle and drove toward the River Clyde. Peter stopped near the water's edge, considered what he'd just done, and threw the pistol into the river. He believed destroying the evidence of the triple killing would keep him out of harm's way should the police, who were always badgering him, came around asking questions.

The move would have worked (destroying the evidence), but later in this terrible tale Peter would confess to these murders (and others) and take police precisely to the spot where he'd dumped the murder weapon. Although two years would span between the killings and when Peter led the police to the location, the gun was actually recovered.

The following morning, Watt family housekeeper, Helen Collison, arrived to clean the house and to visit. While walking up to the house, she noticed the curtains were still drawn and found the rear door locked - these facts she found odd because the Watt family were normally early risers and always left the rear door unlocked because they expected her.

As she got close to the side kitchen door, she saw one of the panes of glass in the door was broken. She began to get worried after noticing the broken glass. Instead of going inside, Helen walked over to a neighbor's house to ask for help. Around the same time, the local postman, Peter Collier, saw Helen and could see she was distraught. She quickly told him what she'd seen and showed him the broken glass pane.

Mr. Collier reached inside the broken glass and unlocked the door. Helen cautiously went inside. In less than a minute, she came back out trembling and confused. She told Mr. Collier that Marion Watt and her sister, Margaret were dead inside of apparent gunshot wounds. As the shock set in, Helen recalled the family had a seventeen-year-old daughter, Vivienne. Helen went back inside and directly to Vivienne's room. She came back out shaking her head, confused, hurt, and scared. She told Mr. Collier that Vivienne was also dead. Mr. Collier helped Helen call the police and waited with her until they arrived.

A triple homicide in any location

(especially in the 1950s when we were all far less desensitized to killing), regardless of the circumstances, can cause panic and fear for residents in the area of the crime. Panic and concern also spreads within the police department tasked to investigate such an atrocity.

The scene was digested by investigators slowly and methodically. They noticed someone had systematically murdered two defenseless women and a female teenager after breaking into their home. The suspect(s) used a pistol to kill the victims. Inspectors didn't need a coroner or forensic investigator to tell them the cause of death based on the obvious bullet holes in all three victims. The crime scene, as told by Detective Superintendent Alexander Brown, had an eerie feeling to it, and those on scene wondered if the killer stumbled upon the victims and killed them or broke into the home specifically to kill them. Brown was the first to notice pictures in the home with a man he assumed was the head of the Watt household. He pointed at one of the photos and declared, "We need to find Mr. Watt."

Police learned from Helen that William Watt, a master baker in Glasgow, was away on a fishing trip. He'd asked Mrs. Watt's sister to come stay with the family while he was fishing. While on scene, police were contacted by a nearby resident advising them that his bungalow, located at 5 Fennbank Avenue, had also been burglarized during the night.

An officer was dispatched to 5 Fennbank Avenue and, almost immediately upon arriving, identified the handiwork used during the burglary as done by Peter Manuel. This fact alone, and Peter's extensive criminal history, made him a person of interest in the Watt family murders.

A massive manhunt for the killer(s) began throughout the area. However, police had very little evidence at the scene. They knew the house was broken into by force, items were stolen, and they had three victims. Other than that, nothing was found giving them any insight to who the killer(s) might be. Also, investigators had a difficult time imagining what motive would exist to kill two women and a child in cold blood.

Glasgow City Police quickly confirmed that William Watt, the man in the pictures, was in fact still on a fishing trip. Initially, the fact he was not home and the police could not get a hold of him right away caused some concern by Superintendent Brown. As such, and the fact they had no other leads at the time (except for the outside chance Peter Manuel was involved based on the home being burgled), William Watt was considered a suspect in the murders of his own family. Police determined they needed to find him right away and were convinced he would know something about the murders. However, more than a few investigators on scene had thoughts of another dangerous man in town.

Local law enforcement was aware that Peter, a prolific home burglar and man with a nasty temper, was known to frequent the area. A records check revealed that Peter was out on bail for yet another burglary at a colliery. He was initially labeled as a person of interest for the burglary at the Watt home, and police wanted to talk to him, but their primary focus was William Watt.

It should be noted that as the Watt family murder case unfolded, Peter was convicted of a burglary at a local colliery and sentenced to eighteen months in prison. This left police to focus on Mr. Watt, but they kept the name of Peter Manuel in the back of their minds.

As the Watt family murder investigation took shape, police located and arrested William Watt for the murders. The shock of first learning his family had been murdered and then being charged for those murders made William queasy. He immediately denied any involvement, but police were adamant he had to be involved.

Glasgow City Police speculated that William could have driven ninety miles (the distance from the fishing area) late through the night, staged an apparent break-in and burglary at his own home, and then murdered his family. Police said he could have done so and returned to Ardrishaig without too many people knowing or seeing him.

A ferryman, employed by Renfrew Ferry, told police initially that he'd seen William Watt on the ferry on the night of the murders. Even though this was not the quickest way to get from Ardrishaig to the Watt residence, police said he must have been up to no good traveling late at night and in the direction of his home. These types of assumptions and theories based on hunches are what get innocent people arrested and found guilty in court.

Police located a motorist who also reported seeing William Watt as they passed each other on Loch Lomondside. This suggested once again that William was traveling throughout the night and could have been the one to kill his family.

When police showed the two witnesses an "identity parade," what American police call a "line up," both witnesses positively picked out William Watt.

Based on the preliminary investigation and the statement of the motorist and Ferryman, William was remanded into custody and lodged in the Barlinnie Prison. For two months he remained locked behind bars, unable to grieve for the loss of his entire family, while Peter Manuel, the real killer, was not considered a suspect.

William would later be set free, however, after police determined that the ferryman's story changed over time and he could not recall the vehicle William was allegedly driving the night his family was murdered.

William maintained his innocence the entire time and for a period (and completely understandable) was described by prison staff as "losing his mind." I cannot imagine having to go through what William Watt went through. Investigators tried to pin the murders on him, but they had to admit his alibi checked out and there was no motive for him to want to kill his family. The most inflammatory information police uncovered pertaining to William was that he had cheated on his wife several times with several different women. Although his adulterous behavior would not be accepted by many people, police knew convincing a jury that he killed his family because he was cheating on his wife would not go well.

The general public remained concerned on several levels after the police let it be known that they were considering the release of William Watt. In an effort to convince the residents that the police were not making a huge mistake, they divulged several pieces of their investigation. Police explained that they'd used frogmen to search the Crinan Canal near where William was staying (in a hotel for the fishing trip) and did not locate a murder weapon or bloody clothing that they were looking for. Likewise, police noted that gas (petrol) levels in William's car had not decreased on the night of the murders, indicating he probably did not drive the vehicle on the evening of the murder.

As police wrestled with the fate of William Watt, Peter Manuel, based on an appeal he won, was released early from custody. Unfortunately, as soon as he exited the prison grounds, he began plotting his next murderous spree.

William Watt could have easily remained in custody had Peter not continued killing people. It makes me sick to think how close the UK legal system came to trying an innocent man for three murders. One can only imagine what roller coaster of emotions William experienced. How he stayed sane during the process boggles me. Then finally, after spending months in prison for doing nothing wrong, police advised the magistrate that William should be released. William Watt could finally try to gather the pieces of his shattered life and seek time to bereave his loss. A certain law enforcement disaster was narrowly averted in this case, but thankfully, justice worked itself out for Mr. Watt.

Photographer filming the Watt family home.

Crowds gathered to watch William Watt paraded to court assuming he was a ruthless killer.

Superintendent James Hardy considering his next move while trying to answer the public outcry surrounding the triple murders.

The Murder of Sydney Dunn

Newcastle upon Tyne, Northumberland,
England, December 8, 1957

Thirty-six-year-old taxi driver Sydney Dunn,
described as having a great sense of humor
and diligent work ethic, enjoyed his job
immensely. Dunn made casual conversation
with his passengers and had a knack for
keeping them laughing while he drove them
to their destination.

On December 8, 1957, at
approximately 4:25 a.m., Sydney Dunn rolled
through Newcastle upon Tyne along the
River Tyne looking for a fare. After a few
minutes, he saw Peter Manuel, whom he did
not know, walking along the road, and their
eyes met. Peter signaled to the man to come
his way. Dunn pulled over in front of Peter
hoping the man had cash and wished to hire
him.

Peter jumped in Dunn's car and
somewhere along the ride he violently killed
Mr. Dunn by shooting him at point-blank
range. For some unknown reason, Peter also

slit Dunn's throat after he'd killed him. Peter then drove Dunn's car to Edmundbyers, nearly twenty miles from Newcastle, and dumped Dunn's vehicle and his body.

The following morning, a policeman cycling along a moorland road where Peter had dumped Dunn's car, saw a vehicle that had driven into a gully. The officer inspected the car and noticed there wasn't a person inside, but he could see fresh blood on the front seats. The officer reported the suspicious situation to the local police department. Several inspectors were sent to the scene and started to piece together what had happened. The first order of business was finding out who owned the taxi. After that, police needed to find the man and check on his welfare.

Since they couldn't find the owner of the car, and there was a large amount of blood at the scene, and the vehicle was found in a gully, police assumed the car owner was seriously injured - murder had not crossed anyone's mind yet. A grid search was conducted as police searched for the victim or clues as to what happened. Within an hour, police located Sydney Dunn. They were taken aback when they rolled him over and saw that his throat had been slit and he'd been shot from close range.

A crime scene was taped off and an investigation into the murder of Sydney Dunn began. The police had no idea Peter Manuel killed Mr. Dunn or that he'd returned to Lanarkshire immediately after disposing of Mr. Dunn's body and vehicle.

Police spent a significant amount of time trying to collect evidence and compiling a list of violent criminals in the area. However, little evidence was available. After all "normal suspects" were interviewed and cleared of the murder, the murder case of Sydney Dunn sat on a shelf pending new leads or someone coming forward as a witness.

Unfortunately, no one came forward, and it would be almost two years later before a small piece of evidence would be found at the scene that would connect Peter to the murder. Peter would later be tried for this murder, although he'd be dead when the case was heard. We'll touch upon the conclusion of the Sydney Dunn murder as this book unfolds. It's interesting to note that some people familiar with the Peter Manuel serial killer case and the Sydney Dunn murder are still not convinced Peter was his killer.

The Murder of Isabelle Cooke

Mount Vernon, Glasgow, Scotland, December 28, 1957

Isabelle Cooke

This time of year, the ground and foliage in Mount Vernon, located in the eastern end of Glasgow, was covered in snow. Middle-class and some wealthy families called the quaint town home.

On December 28, 1957, seventeen-year-old Isabelle Cooke and her friends prepared for a dance at the Uddingston Grammar School scheduled to begin at 6 p.m. She'd made plans to meet her boyfriend at his house and the two would walk to the dance together. After getting the right dress picked out, Isabelle set off to her boyfriend's house. Somewhere along the path to his house, an evil man intervened and snatched her.

There's no way Isabelle could have known her fate or the fact that Peter Manuel had seen her and immediately began stalking her. Peter followed her for a time in his car, then parked and got out. He knew a place just up the road that would be suitable for what he planned to do next.

As Isabelle rounded the bend and came upon a more wooded and desolate location, Peter came unglued and unable to control himself. He lunged and grabbed Isabelle from behind. He quickly dragged her off the beaten path and threw her to the ground. As he'd done while killing Anne Kneilands (recall she too was seventeen years old and headed to a dance when Peter killed her), Peter lost all control of himself and strangled his victim. He then sexually assaulted her after he strangled her to death.

Unlike how he'd left Anne in the same place where he'd killed her, this time he dragged and carried Isabelle to a field close by. It's unclear how, but Peter dug a hole and buried Isabelle in a shallow grave. The secluded location eluded law enforcement detection over the weeks they looked for her after she was reported missing. If it weren't for Peter taking the police to her precise burial location, they may have never found Isabelle.

The fact Isabelle had been murdered was not known right away. At approximately 9 a.m., her father reported her missing to the Glasgow City Police, and she was considered "missing" for quite some time.

Police learned a short time later that Isabelle never made it to the dance, and although she'd been somewhat rebellious as a teenager, no one believed she would miss the dance or meeting up with her boyfriend. Law enforcement, based on these facts and the fact she was a teenager, ruled her "missing case" as suspicious. They did not think Isabelle was playing games with her parents and honestly hoped one of her friends or their parents would call the Cooke family to let them know she was with them.

Remember that police did not know

where Isabelle was, and therefore, they did not know she'd been sexually assaulted and murdered by Peter Manuel. The Glasgow City Police left the case open and spent some time looking for Isabelle, as did her parents, family, and friends. A few of her clothing items were found the following day, near where Peter had abducted and murdered her. Her "missing person" case grew stranger by the day.

Like thousands of missing juvenile reports that are reported daily around the globe, Isabelle's case started to fizzle out within a few weeks. The more time that went by, the more concerned law enforcement grew that Isabelle wasn't missing but rather suspected she might have been murdered. They cited the fact that some of her clothing was located, suggesting foul play and an untimely demise for the young girl.

Police, and Isabelle's family, would not have any answers regarding her status until almost a full year passed. Her parents, family, and friends never gave up hope that she was still alive.

In a bizarre game of cat and mouse, Peter Manuel actually gave Constable Robert

Smith a ride to help search for Isabelle Cooke. This occurred on January 2, 1958, only a few days after Peter murdered her. Obviously her murder was a terrible tragedy and completely unacceptable, but Peter somehow found a way to be even more evil. He drove Constable Smith around looking for the girl he killed. Peter toyed with the inspector, further demonstrating how manipulative and conniving he could be.

The Smart family Murders

Uddingston, South Lanarkshire, Scotland, January 1, 1958

The Hogmanay in Uddingston at the Smart family home, by all accounts, was the typical celebration - complete with tasty treats from Tunnock's. Peter, aged 45, Doris, aged 42, and their son Michael, aged 10, celebrated by eating well, staying up late, and looking forward to the New Year. In the very early hours on January 1st, the family locked up the home, and went to bed.

A few hours later, Peter Manuel, a career criminal and serial killer, selected their home as his next target. He'd considered another home in the area, but when he was caught peering into the house, the homeowner, Mr. McMunn, yelled to his wife to get his gun, forcing Peter to flee. Peter was not the sort of man looking for a gunfight. He'd much rather deal with a home that was unoccupied rather than one where people were home which would cause a problem.

Skilled in breaking and entering, he easily forced his way into the Smart home. Once inside, he fished out his Beretta firearm that he'd bought from Tony Lowe (another career criminal in the UK) and began looking for items to steal. During his hunt for jewelry and other valuable items, he stumbled upon the residents of the home fast asleep. He most likely could have taken food and expensive items from the home without being detected. Instead, Peter Manuel chose to kill more innocent people.

Peter located Mr. and Mrs. Smart asleep in their bedroom. Just as he'd done with the Watt family, Peter shot and killed both of them while they lay in their bed asleep. He then searched the rest of the house for anyone else who might be home and heard the gunshots. Down the hall, he located their son, Michael. Without hesitation, as he had grown accustomed to, Peter shot and killed young Michael while he trembled in his bed. As if murdering three innocent people wasn't enough, Peter managed to become even more sadistic by what he chose to do next.

For almost a week after he'd gunned down the Smart family, Peter remained in their home. He dined on leftovers from the Hogmanay, and later said he enjoyed feeding the family's cat. He slept in their beds after pushing their bodies onto the floor. He used the facilities and watched television as though he was living in his own home. Peter somehow blocked out their images and carried on as though everything was normal.

The story of the attempted break-in at the McMunn's home fueled a growing tension in the neighborhood, especially since it was not common for burglars to pick the neighborhood as a target location. Neighbors, later interviewed when Mr. and Mrs. Smart and their son were discovered, told police they felt, although providing little reason as to why, that something was not right at the Smart home. Some mentioned the curtains at the house were closed all the time. One man said while he studied the home looking for signs of people inside, he had an odd feeling as though he was being watched. Still, no one called the police to report their suspicions that something wasn't right.

At some point, Peter grew bored with his situation. He decided it was time to leave the Smart home. While he rummaged the home for any last tidbits to steal, Peter came across a stack of fresh banknotes Mr. Smart had been saving for a planned family holiday. He pocketed the notes and formulated a plan to leave under the cover of darkness. He noticed car keys in the house and stole the Smarts' vehicle. After driving a short distance, Peter decided the police would be looking for the murderer (him) and his victims' missing car, so he dumped it (similar to the way he dumped Sydney Dunn's taxi).

South Lanarkshire Police had no idea the Smart family had been murdered. Some of the officers later recalled seeing Peter Manuel in the area, but did not stop him because they had no reason to. They were dealing with the missing person case of Isabelle Cooke, and contacting Peter really was the last thing on their minds. Local residents demanded to know where Isabelle Cooke was and wanted answers. However, at that time, police simply had no answers and were just as frustrated as the people they served.

It truly is an empty feeling as a law enforcement member when you cannot provide the answers concerned family members are looking for. As time wore on and Isabelle hadn't been located, police were beginning to believe she'd been killed. However, revealing that hunch to a grieving and scared family would have been catastrophic. Obviously the police continued to look for Isabelle, but even greater known crimes were about to unfold causing them to divert their forces.

As noted previously, Peter remained in the local area and by chance came across Constable Smith. Peter offered the man a ride for several hours as Mr. Smith looked for Isabelle Cooke. Smith later advised that during their discussion in Peter's car, Peter told him that he (Peter) believed the police were not searching the right locations for Isabelle. Only after Peter was caught and his sensationalized trial began, did Constable Smith realize how brazen Peter had become, and on some level he (Smith) was happy he survived his encounter with Peter Manuel. Peter was armed at the time Mr. Smith was in his car. For all the times he'd been contacted and arrested by police and served prison time, it's a miracle he did not take out his complete disdain for police by killing Constable Smith.

As a deputy sheriff with numerous investigations under my belt, many of which were murder cases, I think Peter was playing with law enforcement during this time. Similar to other notable serial killers, Peter stayed in the area and observed what law enforcement was doing trying to identify and capture him. With all my experience, training, and research, I've learned that certain serial killers hang around and socialize with police because they think themselves so superior to the "stupid" cops and enjoy toying with them while believing they will get away with it. Police work, the criminal getting bored or making a mistake, and sometimes blind luck leads to these killers getting apprehended, or killed in the process of getting apprehended.

Peter was quite intelligent and likely could have fled without being caught (at least for some time) but chose to remain. He took this tragic saga a step further by giving Constable Smith a ride and telling him the police were looking in the wrong spot for Isabelle. Either Peter's mind had completely gone distorted or he enjoyed the rush of being so close to the police and them not having any idea they were riding around with a serial killer. Not too many law enforcement members can say they've driven a serial killer around. Those involved in the Peter Manuel serial killer case admitted they would not want to experience meeting and riding around with a serial killer.

The fact Peter killed so easily and was so calm about it solidified him as one of the most ruthless serial killers I've ever researched. His willingness to taunt law enforcement after killing three innocent people demonstrated just how completely gone Peter Manuel was. His past life experience of breaking and entering, sexual assault, stalking, and serial killing made him more sophisticated than most of the law enforcement at the time were prepared for.

On January 6th, when Peter Smart did not return to work after the new year, one of his co-workers called the police to report that it was not like him to miss work without telling someone first. Lanarkshire Police decided to go to Mr. Smart's home to see if they could locate him.

On the way to his home, an officer located Peter Smart's vehicle abandoned just a few blocks from his house. The fact that a co-worker had reported an issue with Peter Smart and his vehicle had been located abandoned away from the home caused the police concern. Two officers went to the Smart bungalow and forced entry into the residence through the back door. There they discovered the horrific murder site of Mr. and Mrs. Smart and their son Michael.

Once news of the Smart family murders broke, the community grew furious, scared, and outraged. Add in the suspicious missing person case of Isabelle Cooke and the triple-murder of the Watt family, and it's easy to see why residents were both extremely concerned and honestly terrified.

Law enforcement felt confident that they were doing everything they could to catch the suspect(s) and find Isabelle, but after the Smart family murders, even the most pessimistic person felt as though a serial killer was loose in the United Kingdom. The fact the serial killer was targeting families and young girls made things even more drastic.

As with the other murders, Peter Manuel's name came up with regard to the Smart family murders. Police were desperate to find the killer(s) and were beginning to believe Peter had involvement in some or all of the killings. However, the fact he'd given police a ride to look for Isabelle Cooke caused some to pause and wonder if he was, in fact a serial killer, why would he do such a thing?

The Smart family home was turned upside down by investigators and a forensic specialist looking for evidence. It was difficult work and not much evidence was collected. Police made several newspaper appeals and news broadcasts advising people to remain calm and protect themselves in their own homes. They also asked anyone with any information about the killings to come forward. The community and local law enforcement officials were in a bit of a tail-spin. It wouldn't be until January 13, 1958, that the big break police were searching for fell squarely into their laps.

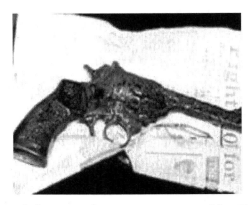

One of the murder weapons used by Peter

Good Old Fashioned Police Work

Glasgow, Scotland, January 13, 1958

Peter Manuel, with a pocket full of stolen banknotes from the Smart family robbery and killings, found himself visiting bars throughout Glasgow and living somewhat of the lavish life. Many of the bartenders and owners knew him, and they knew he was a criminal and rarely had a lot of money. Peter, normally trying to get someone to buy him a drink, was now paying for rounds in the bars he visited, causing concern for patrons and bar owners alike. Bartenders are some of the most perceptive people I've ever met. Their livelihood involves engaging with patrons, in this case, the fact that Peter had a significant change in his behavior registered with them and caused concern and speculation.

One evening, a bartender took it upon himself to call the police. He reported the strange behavior that Peter had been displaying and noted that not only was he (Peter) buying rounds for people, but he was paying with brand new "crisp" banknotes.

The same bartender, perhaps a budding detective himself, kept two of the banknotes Peter had given him when he paid for drinks. The banknotes were later provided to the police and led to the massive break in the cases that police desperately needed.

Investigators were not aware at the time that Mr. Smart had cashed a check and obtained a decent amount of banknotes from his bank. They also did not know that Mr. Smart had hidden the cash at his house, and planned to use it for a family vacation. Lastly, they did not know that Peter had located and stolen the banknotes after he murdered the entire family.

With the banknotes from the bar in hand, police tried to track down where the notes had come from. They too recognized that the banknotes looked new and noted that they had sequential numbering on them. While at a bank, the teller examined the serial numbers of the notes and told police the ones they had were recently given to Mr. Smart. The fact Peter Manuel had in his possession banknotes belonging to Mr. Smart made him the primary suspect in their murders. Those involved in the case were ecstatic, but they had to make sure they followed protocol and procedure with this new information to ensure any case against Peter would not be thrown out later in court due to a rushed mistake.

Several investigators prepared and later showed an identification parade to pub patrons and employees in various pubs in Glasgow. Those shown the parade identified Peter Manuel as the person who used banknotes in the same sequence as the ones provided to Peter Smart. The witnesses also told the same story; Peter was buying people drinks when he used to beg for a pint.

Armed with this damaging evidence connecting Peter to the murders of Peter, Doris, and Michael Smart, police began searching for him while a search warrant was written for him and where he lived - his parents' home. All of the witness statements, the banknotes, the bank records, and the officer's opinion led to developing enough probable cause to secure a search warrant.

On January 13, 1958, nine officers responded to Peter's parents' home with a search warrant in hand. They demanded entry and forced the door open. They detained Mr. and Mrs. Manuel and Peter. They searched the home for key pieces of evidence such as more banknotes, Smart family house keys, and any other items of evidence connecting Peter to the break-in and murders.

Police began fielding questions from Mr. Manuel. He was furious that the police were in his home. Peter originally was quiet, but as his dad began to challenge the police, Peter found himself chiming in. Nevertheless, the detectives located more banknotes, keys, and an electric razor they believed connected Peter to the Smart family break-in and murders.

Peter was removed from his parents' home and placed under arrest. He was transported back to the Hamilton Police station, a location that would become pivotal in the serial killer's eventual demise.

Before he was handcuffed and removed from the house, Peter had already formulated a plan and an explanation for why police found evidence in his room. His experienced and cold mind convinced himself that he could out-fox the police once again.

His mother could not bear to see her

son be led away in handcuffs. Mr. and Mrs. Manuel were not entirely sure what Peter was being charged with, but the fact homicide inspectors were at their home indicated Peter was in big trouble. They did not know right away that their son would later be labeled as one of the UK's most prolific serial killers.

A few hours later, after Peter was already at the station, his parents arrived and demanded to speak to their son. Police were not willing to allow the visit and were concerned, since his arrest and subsequent trial would likely be a capital murder case, that any contact Peter had with his parents might convince him not to talk to the police. Also, there was an initial thought by law enforcement that Peter's father could somehow be involved with the murders or with trying to hide that his son had done them.

In a case of such magnitude, and as the layers of Peter Manuel's disgusting actions became clear, his arrest seemed almost anti-climactic given his level of sophistication and the fact he was a brutal serial killer. As is the case with many serial killer cases, it seemed as though Peter was exhausted and no longer had much left up his sleeve with regard to trying to fool the police. In a weird way, Peter did not put up much of a fight because he wanted to tangle with police in court.

Police were certain of his involvement in the Smart family killings, but had not yet been confident of his association to other murders in the area. As they prepared a manner in which to attack his character and question him about other murders in the area, Peter spontaneously told them that he had plenty to say about more than the Smart family. In fact, within a few days of being apprehended for their murders, Peter began to tell his disgustingly eerie tales and told police, in the form of a confession, of many murders he'd committed.

In all, he'd write over three hundred and forty confessions with regard to his serial killing, break-ins, and other crimes. It should be noted, though, that as time and the investigation wore on, Peter would allege he was coerced into his confessions (we will explore this in great detail later) and would attempt to withdraw them completely. The fact of the matter was, raw evidence tied him initially to the Smart family murders and several other break-ins (including the Watt family home) that would help police confirm Peter was responsible for several brutal and unbelievable crimes over the last two years. However, even hardened investigators at the Hamilton Police station were not prepared for what he was about to tell them.

Peter was afforded a few minutes with his parents basically in the hallway of the police station on the day he was arrested during the service of the search warrant. He looked at them and said, "It's difficult to tell you things, it's always been difficult to speak to you freely." His parents nodded and his mother began to become extremely emotional. Peter and his father looked at each other, but did not talk for over a minute. The tension hung in the police station like Los Angeles smog.

Peter broke the silence, "There is no future for me. I have done some terrible things." His parents, who could have not known what their son was talking about, seemed to understand they'd lost their son for good. His mother could not stand seeing Peter in anguish and convinced her husband that they needed to leave. They left the station but would soon return as a three day long confession and intense investigation ensued.

As his parents left the station, Peter turned and looked at one of the inspectors and produced an evil-looking grin. He later said that he decided at that moment that he would toy with the police, like he did when he drove Constable Smith around while looking for Isabelle Cooke. He made up his mind to manipulate the situation until he grew bored again.

However, police were so familiar with Peter at the time that they placed him in a holding cell for almost twenty-two hours and did not allow him to speak to anyone. The plan was a result of the inspectors knowing Peter craved attention. They felt keeping him on ice and not letting him know everything that was happening would get him to talk more openly. Peter figured out their plan after a few hours and decided to play along. However, many hours later, he grew frustrated and wanted to keep the game going, so he decided he would slowly provide the police with great details for what he'd done to the Watt family, Isabelle Cooke, Anne Kneilands, and the Smart family.

The fact Peter could manipulate so

many other intelligent people speaks about his mental capacity and his own high level of intelligence. He never finished high school and his IQ was never officially tested, but people involved in his case were adamant that he was not just some street thug. We see high intelligence quite often in the world of serial killers, but we've seen many other factors that contributed to Peter Manuel becoming one of the worst serial killers the UK would ever experience.

Confessions of a Serial Killer

Glasgow, Scotland, January 16, 1958

Peter was provided paper and pencil and he began writing feverishly, listing all of his sins. He continued to write and would take small breaks as his hand began to cramp. Without provocation, he told them that he'd killed Anne Kneilands (which was a terrific shock for those involved with her murder case and the investigators at the station) and openly admitted to killing the Smart family.

Police gently reminded him that it was in his best interest to tell the whole story, and he continued to write it out. Strangely, police reports indicate specifically that Peter was offered an attorney or representation several times during this key point in this case (and his sick life). He refused each time.

Some of you reading this may wonder why the police were trying, in some respects, to help a serial killer. The reason is, even though they had their man in custody, the true test for the investigators would occur in court when the case was presented. By continually offering Peter an attorney, and documenting his refusal, it safe-guarded the police and clearly showed they were not attempting to violate Peter's rights. Had they received the information and confessions and not offered Peter an attorney, everything he said could be tossed out during the pending court trial. In addition, if the police, as they did in this case, were able to find evidence (murder weapons, a buried victim, banknotes, and other vastly important items for this case), every one of those items could also be thrown out of court. It turned out in this case, which we will examine further in later chapters, Peter would claim he was forced to write all of the confessions and demanded that the evidence and confessions be dismissed against him. He later fired his attorney and represented himself for the remainder of his murder trial.

Apprehending a murder suspect is truly only the beginning of any case, especially when it comes to serial killers who've killed nine innocent people. The fact the investigators offered Peter an attorney in the infancy of the investigation and documented his refusals literally saved their case. Had they not done so, and been completely thorough with this point, it is very likely every one of his confessions would not have been included in the case against him. The Crown would have had to disallow them for violating Peter's rights.

Police, now on a roll and hopeful they could solve several similar murders or suspected murders within the general area, asked Peter if he knew anything about the whereabouts of Isabelle Cooke. He looked up from writing and told them he did in fact know about her murder. This caught the attention of the investigators because, up until that moment, it was not official that her suspicious missing person case might also have been a murder case.

Well into the night, Peter agreed to take the detectives to where Isabelle could be found. He was driven to a recently ploughed field where he told the driver to stop and pull over. Peter, led by the detectives and handcuffed, walked into the field. At one point, one of the detectives stopped as did Peter. The detective, skeptical that Peter was telling the truth about knowing where Isabelle was, looked at Peter and asked, "Where is Isabelle?"

Peter smiled and replied, "You're standing on her."

The detectives called for a forensic specialist and more investigators to their location. Within an hour, the remains of Isabelle Cooke, decomposed from over a year in the earth, were located and Peter was charged with her abduction and murder. One of the detectives noted in his report how gruesome and bizarre Peter seemed at the precise moment he told them they were standing over Isabelle's gravesite. It was as though Peter was reliving the violent confrontation and gaining some sort of enjoyment from an incident that occurred over a year prior.

Police put Peter back in a squad car and drove him back to the Hamilton Police station. Once there, Inspector Matthew Cleland, Lanarkshire Police, was asked to babysit him as more leads (that Peter had provided) were being investigated.

For some reason, Peter took a liking to Cleland and asked him for more paper and pencil. During this time, Peter wrote the longest and most accurate (also the most challenged statement in the subsequent court hearings) confession regarding Anne Kneilands, the Smart family, Isabelle Cooke, and the Watt family. Cleland read the confession, and called several inspectors back to the station for further follow-up.

Peter asked to speak to his parents. This time, the police decided not to let him. Peter later claimed that the police coerced him into writing more confessions and used his parents as leverage to force him to show them places he'd just written about in his last confession. Peter did not like that the police were not letting him see his parents, but for the time being, they had him dead to rights.

After brief negotiations, which included the police telling Peter he could see his parents after he provided them more evidence against him, Peter agreed to take the detectives to key locations.

First, they responded to the River Clyde, where Peter pointed out where their frogman could dive and would locate a gun used in the murders. Peter then told them to drive to the area of General's Bridge. When asked why, he told them he'd thrown Anne Kneilands' underwear and the piece of iron he used to kill her off the bridge. Once these locations were marked and authorities were called to the locations, Peter said he had more to show the inspectors.

They drove, while Peter discussed what he'd been doing the last two years, toward an area where he used to hide while watching Anne Kneilands. He pointed to a Gas Board shed, near to Anne's home, and told them to stop the car. Peter and the detectives exited the vehicle and walked toward the shed. He told them he hid the clothing he wore when he killed her in the shed for quite some time, but later burned the evidence so it could not be used against him.

At each new location, and while new evidence against Peter was being obtained, police stopped and advised him he could have counsel present if he chose so. Time and time again, Peter refused and explained that he wanted to get all that he'd done off his chest. It became clear to the investigators that Peter enjoyed all of the attention he was given while working with the police to solve the murders he committed. In some respects, it also seemed as though Peter was gaining some satisfaction at getting all of the murders off his chest - he wasn't sorry for what he did, but divulging them gave his head less things to think about.

Ultimately, Peter would have visits with his parents several times between January 13th and January 17, 1958. Oddly, he did not disclose to them anything he'd done, but just kept telling them that he had made mistakes. His parents were so confused and hurt that the visits were fewer and shorter as the days wore on. Peter loved his parents more than anything, but he hadn't built the courage to tell them how terrible he was and what he'd done.

Peter would later claim that the investigators told him they would arrest his whole family (his parents and sister) and send them to prison unless he confessed to the killings. He noted that he loved his parents and sister and maintained that they had nothing to do with any of the crimes he'd committed. He was quoted as saying, "I confessed to the murders to keep my family out of all of this." The fact the police were willing to drag his family into the situation (a point adamantly denied by all of the officers and inspectors while testifying in the case) upset Peter immensely, but he had to internalize the fact that he'd said too much already, and an unbelievable strong showing in court would be required to convince the Crown to set him free. Even though Peter felt he was still calling all the shots and in complete control of his situation, he had almost certainly sealed his fate because of his arrogance.

Officers searching an area Peter Manuel told them they'd find evidence of his killings.

Detectives stand with a frogman after locating the weapon Peter used to kill the Smart family.

The Circus Comes to Town

Residents waited in line for hours to witness the trial of Peter Manuel.

Peter escorted to court, 1958.

Glasgow, Scotland, May 12, 1958

The United Kingdom's most anticipated criminal case charging a serial killer in the murders of eight people (Sydney Dunn was not considered at this time) drew quite a spectacle. Residents, largely set at ease with the announcement of Peter Manuel being captured and charged with several murders, were compelled to stand in long lines for hours hoping to get a glimpse of him and to be a part of the extremely well-publicized trial.

Lord Cameron, an experienced judge, had his hands full when the prosecution team, Peter Manuel, and a bevy of defense attorneys finally took their seats that first day of open court. Local residents and the media filled the room completely, and there was a buzz floating around stirring a wide variety of emotions.

Within minutes, Harold Leslie, a well-known and properly schooled attorney, was appointed by the Crown to represent alleged serial killer Peter Manuel. Reporters at the time noted that Peter looked Mr. Leslie up and down, smiled, and nodded his head, seemingly approving the Crown's appointment. The working relationship, however, did not last long. Among the many reasons the union failed was the fact Peter was impossible to represent and Mr. Leslie never truly had his heart in defending a sadistic serial killer.

Nevertheless, the proceedings began with the list of charges being read against Peter. I found it interesting that the prosecution included lesser crimes, such as breaking and entering, when charging him initially. However, if the prosecution could prove the burglaries into the Smart family and Watt family homes were committed by Peter, it would be much easier to convince a jury that he also killed the families inside those homes. It makes more sense that someone who burglarized a home while the victims were asleep likely killed them rather than one person breaking in and another completely random person committing six completely senseless murders.

Charge #1 - That on or about January 2, 1956, Peter Manuel murdered Anne Kneilands.

Charge #2 - That on or about September 16, 1956, Peter Manuel broke into the Platt family home and took numerous items, including an electric razor.

Charge #3 - That on or about September 17, 1956, Peter Manuel broke into the Watt family home located on Fennsbank Avenue.

Charge #4 - That on or about September 17, 1956, Peter Manuel murdered Vivienne Watt,

Marion Watt, and Margaret Brown.

Charge #5 - That on or about December 25, 1957, Peter Manuel broke into a home in Mt. Vernon and took numerous items.

Charge #6 - That on or about December 28, 1957, Peter Manuel stalked, sexually assaulted, and murdered Isabelle Cooke.

Charge #7 - That on or about January 1, 1958, Peter Manuel broke into the Smart family home.

Charge #8 - That on or about January 1, 1958, Peter Manuel killed Peter, Doris, and Michael Smart.

Charge #9 - That on or about January 7, 1958, Peter Manuel stole a vehicle belonging to the Smart family.

The charges against Peter were many, but the prosecutor was armed with volumes of police reports to support the probable cause for the charges. Still, a rather lengthy court battle (costing hundreds of thousands of dollars) would be necessary in order for the prosecution team to successfully convict Peter Manuel of eight murders, six of which were capital murder charges.

Mr. Leslie advised the Crown that his client wished to plead not guilty. This claim concerned the investigating officers present in court, as well as the prosecutor, because they had hundreds of pages entered as evidence that were written by Peter indicating that he alone had killed the victims.

During the next eight days of court, Leslie would offer the following statements and evidence attempting to show that his client was in fact innocent. To do so, Peter himself would go on the stand and attempt his greatest manipulation with the men and women of the jury. While many would be nervous and scared while on the hot seat, Peter commanded the role and found himself aroused as everyone was held captive to every word he uttered.

With regard to Charge #1, Peter

admitted he worked in East Kilbride on January 4, 1956, and learned on the same date that a girl had been killed and her body located in Caplerig (It was his victim, Anne Kneilands). Approximately one week after learning about Kneilands' death, Peter met Superintendent Hendry of Lanarkshire CID and recalled that Mr. Hendry contacted him. Peter said Mr. Hendry asked him if he'd been in East Kilbride in the last few weeks. Peter maintained that he told Mr. Hendry, "No." Peter then said Mr. Hendry told him that a female bus driver said she saw him (Peter) in East Kilbride around the time Anne Kneilands had been murdered.

Based on the bus driver's statement, Mr. Hendry detained Peter and they both drove to Peter's place (his parents' home). Mr. Hendry took some clothing from Peters' room and drove both of them back to the police station. Peter said he was questioned at length about Anne's murder, but he provided an alibi. He told police that he got into a fight in Glasgow and went drinking the following night (which he said was January 2nd and on to the early hours of the 3rd). Peter said the police had to let him go because he did not kill Anne Kneilands.

On the 14th of January in 1956, Peter said he remembered seeing his picture featured in the Scottish Daily Press. He said even after he was let go by the police a week prior, they were trying to frame him for Anne Kneilands' murder (by posting his face in connection to her murder in the newspaper). Peter (through Mr. Leslie) claimed he was not receiving a fair trial because of moves like this made by the police. Peter contended that he was being framed by corrupt police officers.

With regard to Charge #2, Mr. Leslie stated that Peter Manuel did have an electric razor in his possession, but he claimed he obtained the razor from Charles Tallis. Charles Tallis was a friend of Peter's and also a prolific thief. Of course Mr. Leslie argued that obviously Charles Tallis must have committed the burglary related to Charge #2 and the police needed to find and charge Charles Tallis.

With regard to Charges #3 and #4, Mr. Leslie had a lengthy response that went as follows. His client denied breaking into the Watt family home. Once again, he alleged that Charles Tallis bragged to him about being given a large sum of money to break into the same home, but not to take too many items.

Peter claimed that sometime in July of 1956, he met up with Charles who showed him two .38 caliber handguns. He said he and Tallis discussed breaking into homes and decided to meet up again on September 16, 1956 (one day prior to the Watt family murders). The criminals allegedly planned to meet at the Woodend Hotel.

On September 16th, Peter showed up and claimed Tallis was a no show. Peter said he waited for several hours and later left with a woman who he could not identify.

Mr. Leslie said on the day of the murders (September 17, 1956), Charles Tallis showed up unannounced at Peter's parents' home. Peter was not home and Charles Tallis left. Peter and Tallis later met up in town at a pub, and Peter told the Crown that he challenged Charles about the triple-murder that happened in town.

On September 18, 1956, Peter told the court that he located a .38 caliber gun, one very similar to the one Charles Tallis had shown him previously, in a drawer in the dining room table at his parents' home. Next to the .38 caliber gun were five empty .38

caliber shell casings. Peter said he looked for Charles for five days to ask him about the gun and shell casings but could not find him.

On September 23, 1956, Peter confronted Charles about the gun and Charles allegedly told him he (Charles) placed it in the drawer. Without further proof or any way to verify the statement, Mr. Leslie advised the Crown that Mr. Watt (recall that he was on a fishing trip at the time his family was killed) admitted to him that he, William Watt, killed his own family.

It should be noted that the prosecution was appalled at the completely idiotic story Peter and his attorney were parading through court as though anyone would find an ounce of truth to it. Lead prosecutor, Gordon Gillies, however, showed great patience. He could see that Peter's recollection of the events, meant to confuse the court and shed doubt as to his involvement in the crimes, was actually working against him. Mr. Gillies was content to play whatever games Mr. Leslie and Peter Manuel had in mind. A few reporters stated that it appeared that Prosecutor Gillies was not convinced and was eager to cross-examine Peter and shred his story to pieces.

With regard to Charge #5, Peter adamantly denied any involvement with a break-in at a home in Mt. Vernon. He offered that he watched a program on boxing at the time the break-in occurred. He did not provide the Crown with the name of the program or what channel it might have been on.

With regard to Charge #6, Mr. Leslie said his client could not have murdered Isabelle Cooke because he was in Glasgow at the time she was killed. This claim was beyond absurd. Peter himself took investigators to a field and had one of them stand directly over Isabelle's grave. How would he know of her precise location if he had not killed her? All of the facts and evidence would come out soon, but the investigators in the courtroom were growing more and more upset by the nonsense being spewed by Mr. Leslie and Peter Manuel. They felt, as they should have, that Peter Manuel was playing with the media and law enforcement and there wasn't much they could do about it - yet.

With regard to Charges #7 and #8, Peter offered an interesting spin on the Smart family murders. He claimed that he was actually close friends to the Smart family and had known them since 1953. Peter said sometime prior to December 25, 1957, Mr. Smart asked Peter if he could get him a firearm.

On December 31, 1957, Peter advised the Crown that he met with Mr. Smart at Royal Oak where Peter provided Mr. Smart a .38 caliber handgun. He alleged that Mr. Smart invited him to visit at his home and he took him up on the offer. When he arrived at the Smart family home, he found them all dead. Peter tried to convince the court that it looked like Mr. Smart killed his wife and son, and then killed himself. Peter admitted to taking the gun from Mr. Smart's side and left the home and could not explain why he did not alert the police of what he saw. Peter then tried to correct himself and pled directly to Lord Cameron that it was him (Peter) who called the murders in to the police. Peter reasoned, "Why would I call in the murders if I committed them?"

Finally, in the middle of May 1958, prosecutor Gordon Gillies, who'd kept meticulous notes of the things Peter had said while on the stand, had his opportunity to cross-examine serial killer Peter Manuel. Mr.

Gillies first focused on the hundreds of written confessions Peter had written which were largely used to charge him in the matter before the Crown.

Peter feigned concern and told Mr. Gillies that he provided the confessions, "so the police would leave my family alone." Peter then blurted, "They threatened me to get those confessions." Mr. Gillies would call countless officers at a later date to refute Peter's claim of being coerced or threatened, but he didn't want to play his cards so quickly.

Mr. Gillies informed the jury, while holding a stack of police reports, that the defendant had been offered an attorney several times, over the course of three days, and he refused. He told the Crown that he would place every officer involved in the case on the stand, and all of them would testify that they offered Peter an attorney and he chose not to get one. Satisfied the issue of Peter being threatened or forced to give a confession had been properly addressed, Mr. Gillies ended his presentation.

Defense attorney Leslie made his closing argument about the confessions. He summarized an argument to exclude the confessions, but Lord Cameron directed many aggressive questions directly at Mr. Leslie. Once Mr. Leslie was done, Lord Cameron made a decision. He stated, "Having seen and heard the witnesses, I have no doubt in preferring the denials of the police officers to the assertions of the accused," he paused for a moment then continued, "I have come to the conclusion that no ground has been established for excluding the statements."

This ruling completely crushed Peter's case and marked the first of many victories for the police officers involved in the case and for Prosecutor Gillies.

Prosecutor Gillies briefly questioned Peter regarding the charges before him.

Peter claimed the facial scratches found on him when police contacted him came from a previous fight and advised the Crown that no skin samples were taken from Anne Kneilands or him, so it was not possible to demonstrate whether he was involved or not. This line of reasoning demonstrates clearly that Peter was quite intelligent and capable of thinking of various defenses for the accusations against him.

With regard to the break-in at the Platt house, Peter said the razor police found at his home was there long before the alleged break-in.

With regard to the break-in at the Martin house, Peter claimed his criminal associate, Mr. Tallis, knew the full descriptions of some of the rings taken in the robbery. He added that Mr. Tallis read about the rings in the paper on September 17th, but pointed out that the rings were not publicly known until September 21st. This meant that only the true person who robbed the house would know about a key point such as the rings if they were involved.

With regard to the Watt family murders, Peter conceded that Mr. Watt did not have a motive to kill his family, but he had less of a motive.

With regard to the Houston home break-in, Peter said he was watching television at the time and could give detail on the program he was watching. No one was impressed with this defense ploy.

With regard to the murder of Isabelle

Cooke, Peter now claimed that he was at a cinema at the time she was killed. He chuckled and advised the court that if he killed someone, he'd take the time to make sure no one saw him do so. (An eye witness actually picked him out after he killed Isabelle).

With regard to the Smart family murders, Peter argued with Mr. Gillies and said the link between him and the murders was "extremely thin." He also said to the jury that he was not, "the confessing type," and therefore he would not have simply confessed of his own free will.

Rolling on the cusp of the initial ruling in his favor to keep the confessions, and now the completely ridiculous points Peter attempted to make when discussing the charges, Mr. Gillies turned toward setting the foundation for each of the charges against Peter, beginning with Charge #1. However, the day had been long and time was running out for the day. Court was adjorned and Peter was escorted to his holding cell.

The following day, as court began, Peter Manuel stunned everyone in the room by speaking directly to Lord Cameron. This was highly frowned upon and a great risk for Peter. He abruptly told the judge that he no longer wished to be represented by Mr. Leslie, or any other attorney. As if this wasn't huge news at the moment, Peter further stunned the room when he matter-of-factly explained that from that moment forward, he would represent himself.

Once the shock wore off, a discussion between Lord Cameron, prosecutor Gillies, and Harald Leslie began. Ultimately, Lord Cameron was obligated to advise Peter that it would be in his best interest, given the nature of the case and the serious charges against him, to keep Mr. Leslie as his attorney. Peter refused and advised the Crown that he not only wanted to represent himself, but it was his right to, and he felt he'd do a better job than any attorney. Lord Cameron reminded Peter that if he was found guilty of the charges, he'd be hanged. Peter fully accepted that fact and maintained it was his right to represent himself.

Although Lord Cameron, Mr. Gillies, and Mr. Leslie felt Peter was making a big mistake, they all agreed that he had the right to represent himself. Lord Cameron relieved Mr. Leslie of his duty and acknowledged that

Peter Manuel, an alleged devious serial killer, now represented himself.

*****

Prosecutor Gillies called Detective Inspector Thomas Goodall, Glasgow Police, to the stand to discuss the murder of Isabelle Cooke. Mr. Gillies had already called Detective Inspector Robert McNeil, Lanarkshire Police, regarding Isabelle Cooke, and his statements were submitted without much discussion from Peter Manuel.

Detective Inspector Goodall confirmed that Peter showed him and Detective Inspector McNeil where Isabelle Cooke's body would be found. He added that Peter requested to stay at the location until police could dig up the body. He told Peter that would not likely happen, which made Peter visibly upset. Inspector Goodall said, "He appeared upset and demanded he stay until the body was found." Goodall advised the court that they drove Peter from the scene and he grew even more frustrated. He testified that Peter told him he wanted to write a full statement and mentioned he (Peter) had thrown two guns in the River Clyde. This testimony was damaging against

Peter and set up evidence discovered in other murders in the case.

Peter sat patiently until Prosecutor Gillies was finished with his witness. When it was Peter's turn to cross-examine Inspector Goodall, his face lit up from the joy. He stood up proudly, with everyone's attention on him (which is what he craved). He tried to rule the room with charm and persuasion. Peter asked Inspector Goodall a question about gloves and a camera.

Inspector Goodall told Peter he had no idea what he was talking about. Several chuckles could be heard in the crowd while others had puzzled looks.

Peter then tried to set and spring a trap with his next question. His attorney previously had tried to build a case that the police had framed Peter for Isabelle's murder.

With a serious and accusatory tone, he asked Inspector Goodall, "Before you came to the house, did you know where Isabelle Cooke's body was?"

"Before we came to the house on the 14th? Definitely not," Inspector Goodall replied. He wore his disdain for Peter, and his question, on his face.

"You did not know where her body was?" Peter asked again.

"That is nonsense to suggest it," replied Inspector Goodall.

Peter moved on with witness Inspector Goodall.

"Did you not make a statement that if I confessed to eight murders, I would go down in history?"

"I certainly did not," answered Inspector Goodall.

One wonders if Peter asking the question about 'going down in history' was somehow his own sick desire of being world famous.

Peter then focused on another piece of evidence used against him regarding Isabelle's murder. Previous testimony indicated that Peter had taken Inspector Goodall and Inspector McNeil to a brickyard where piles of bricks were stored. Peter walked directly to one brick, moved it, and there the inspectors found a shoe belonging to Isabelle Cooke.

Peter asked Inspector Goodall, "There would be thousands of bricks scattered?"

"Yes."

"And you contend that in the dark, I just stopped and shoved aside a brick and pulled out a shoe?"

Inspector Goodall nodded, "You did."

"Just in the dark like that?"

"In the dark," Inspector Goodall calmly replied.

It's unclear why Peter decided not to question Inspector Goodall much further regarding this case. Some speculate he did not believe he could get under his skin and continuing to try to trap him in statements was useless. Comfortable with the testimony of Inspector Goodall, Prosecutor Gillies then called Detective Superintendent Alexander Brown, senior Glasgow Police officer.

Mr. Gillies, through Mr. Brown's testimony, reiterated the fact that police responded to Peter's parents' home and arrested him and how, after this occurred, Peter took them to the gravesite of Isabelle Cooke and told police where guns used in the Smart and Watt murders would be located.

Peter then asked Superintendent Brown highly technical questions about firearms. Specifically, he asked him about the recovered Beretta and how it was missing the magazine spring. Peter enjoyed sharing with the court his extensive knowledge about firearms, but did not ask any questions that would help convince the jury he was innocent of the crimes he'd been charged with.

"I am not a firearms expert," is how Superintendent Brown answered most of Peter's questions and his accusation that the Berretta could not be loaded or fired without the magazine spring.

Hoping to demonstrate that the police were setting him up for the murders in the case, Peter began questioning Superintendent Brown regarding the night they came to his father's home and arrested him.

"Is it not a fact that when you came to that house, you already had intentions of taking me from that house as quickly as possible?"

"No, you would have remained in the house if you had conducted yourself properly." Superintendent Brown paused, then added, "You became aggressive and told your father not to allow us to search the house."

"Did you not tell me you were going to hang me for ten murders?"

"I couldn't tell you that."

"Did you threaten me in any way?" Peter asked, still focused on his confessions and how he believed he was threatened to make them. It did not matter as Lord Cameron had already ruled the confessions were valid and they were already entered as evidence against Peter.

"Never, at any time," replied Superintendent Brown.

"Did you threaten to arrest my father and charge him with being involved in the Smart murders?"

"I did not."

Peter went on for almost an hour apparently fixated on the witness, and desperately trying to convince the jury he was forced into making confessions and had nothing to do with the murder of Isabelle Cooke or the Smart family. He did not, at this time, discuss the other charges against him. While representing himself, and basking in the limelight of everyone looking at him when he was talking, Peter failed to see that he was actually damaging his credibility and making matters much worse for him. Based on the fact so many people had testified against him and all seemed credible, Peter's attempts to try to trick them did not go unnoticed by the jury. In fact, most of the jurors would later state that it was clear Peter Manuel lied whenever he opened his mouth.

Several other officers and detectives would be called to testify in the case against Peter Manuel. Each time they'd bring with them more damaging evidence against Peter while he spent most of his time smiling and carrying on in front of the jury and media.

Once Prosecutor Gillies finished with his law enforcement witnesses, he turned to the doctors involved in examining the victims, Professor Andrew Allison and Dr. James Imrie.

*****

Professor Andrew Allison, a forensic medical specialist, was the first on the stand.

He began with his examination of Anne Kneilands.

Dr. Allison noted the place where she died, marked by a large pool of blood, was not where she was found. This indicated that her body had been moved after she was killed. His notes indicated the victim died "of extreme violence" because her head had been smashed in and a large portion of her skull had been shattered.

He stated, "Blood and brain matter had been splattered between seven and eight feet from the victim," indicating excessive force had been used when the victim's head was crushed with a blunt object. An iron bar had been recovered by police, and Dr. Allison demonstrated how it would have been used to kill the victim, but was careful to add that it was not clear that the piece of iron the police had submitted as evidence was the precise instrument the killer used to murder Anne.

The victim's body was also examined for any signs of sexual assault or rape, and none were noted.

Focus then turned to Vivienne Watt. Dr. Allison noted her head and face had marks consistent with being struck with an object, possibly being knocked unconscious, before being shot. He stated, "the unnatural position of her right arm under her body" supported his conclusion that she fell awkwardly when struck, then the murderer shot and killed her.

Dr. Allison testified that the victim's clothing had been ripped off of her and the bullet wound to her head "was such that she might have survived for some time." Marion Watt and Margaret Brown died prior to Vivienne, both from bullet wounds to their heads at close range.

Vivienne's room, unlike where Marion and Margaret were discovered, appeared to have been staged, as items and clothing were moved about and seemed out of place. Dr. Allison suggested the killer did so in an effort to convince the police some sort of struggle had ensued in the room. He went so far to suggest that the killer made some effort to confuse the police when they entered the room, indicating the high level of sophistication of the killer.

Prosecutor Gillies then discussed the murder of Isabelle Cooke. Dr. Allison noted that her bra was wrapped around her neck and "a headscarf had been tied around her head with the knot forced into her mouth." The testimony caused some rumbling by the men and women in the jury box. The cause of Isabelle's death was ruled asphyxiation. Bruising had been found on her face indicating she was struck several times. A vaginal sample was taken and no seminal fluid was found.

The murders of Isabelle Cooke, Anne Kneilands, and Vivienne Watt, as the evidence suggested, were particularly gruesome. The focus then turned to the Smart family.

Based on his evaluation, Dr. Allison stated the cause of death for Peter, Doris, and Michael was gunshot wounds to their heads and noted that their deaths were "immediate, while they were asleep, and they were unafraid."

Police had obtained a jacket and a pair of trousers belonging to Peter Manuel and submitted them as evidence. After evaluating them, Dr. Allison said he located trace amounts of blood on the left jacket pocket and left front trouser pocket, but that he could not perform further tests as the sample was too minute.

One of the defenses Peter suggested in the trial (while still being represented by Mr. Leslie) was that the Smart family and the Watt family committed suicide. When asked about the possibility of any of the murders he investigated being suicides, Dr. Allison denied such an accusation and found the suggestion appalling.

Dr. Allison was asked, "You excluded suicide in all cases?"

"Not in all cases," Dr. Allison replied.

Harald Leslie thought he saw an opening, but then his head sank. "I am obliged to you. Except in the case of the two girls."

Dr. Allison nodded.

Mr. Leslie continued, "Upon what grounds did you rule out suicide?"

"The wounds were actually in a position which is used by many suicides, but when a person shoots himself through the head, he leaves the weapon behind, and had there been suicide in any of the six cases, then one would have expected to find six firearms lying around. There was not one," answered Dr. Allison.

At the time, this testimony was damaging to Peter's case, poking significant holes in his rebuttal that the victims all committed suicide. While sitting in court and listening to Dr. Allison, Peter kept many notes and would nod often. At some point, Peter knew he'd need to explain where all the guns went if anyone was to entertain the thought that the Smart family and Watt family committed suicide. He stashed these thoughts away and would attempt to bring them up later, after he fired Mr. Leslie, and basically when his case was a complete mockery.

Mr. Allison was excused as a witness and Dr. Imrie came to the stand. Within an hour, it was obvious that Dr. Imrie was reiterating precisely what Dr. Allison had just testified to. Dr. Imrie's testimony was short and to the point. In his medical opinion, based on the evidence, the victims were murdered, and the two girls particularly suffered greatly at the hands of Peter Manuel.

The prosecution's case bore on with more information, testimony, facts, and other courtroom details dragging the case along. Eventually, Mr. Gillies rested his presentation to the Crown. Normally, the case would be submitted and the jury would deliberate. However, in one last desperate attempt to speak his mind, Peter asked Lord Cameron if he could address the jury directly.

Lord Cameron mulled the request and asked Mr. Gillies if he objected. At this point, Mr. Gillies saw no reason to object to Peter's request. It appeared anytime Peter opened his mouth, it worked to the prosecution's advantage. Therefore, Peter's request to speak directly to the jury was granted.

Peter stood, adjusted his suit, and began to tell the jury he had nothing to do with the murders in the case against him. However, he did acknowledge (the first time since writing it out in a confession) breaking into the homes of the Smart family and the Watt family. We'll never know why Peter felt admitting to being at the crime scenes of horrific murders benefited him. In certain aspects of his defense, Peter demonstrated a solid grasp of presenting a case in court; this, however, was a grave error. After thirty or so minutes of his plea to the jury, largely fueled by his self-loathing and pausing several times to grab the attention of the press, he sat down and advised the Crown that he was finished.

On May 29, 1958, Lord Cameron read the jury instructions to the men and women on the jury. They were long because there were so many charges. In addition, because the prosecution was seeking the death penalty against Peter, special instructions were required. In an interesting twist in this case, Lord Cameron essentially threw out the case against Peter as it pertained to the murder of Anne Kneilands.

The Crown told the jury that they must not find Peter Manuel guilty of her murder due to the lack of evidence. Everyone in the courtroom, even Peter himself, was stunned by Lord Cameron's statement. Sadly, the family and friends of Anne Kneilands, and the prosecution and law enforcement, knew Peter had killed Anne. To hear the judge outright order the jury to find Peter not guilty was a crushing blow to those involved.

Soon thereafter, the jury was sent off to a secluded area to deliberate on the case they'd heard for the last twelve days. In less than two hours, the jury reached a unanimous decision and advised Lord Cameron that they were prepared to read the verdicts. The jury was escorted back into the courtroom and the tension in the room skyrocketed. The jury foreman rose and advised the Crown of the following verdicts:

With regard to charge 1: Murder of Anne Kneilands, NOT GUILTY. With regard to charge 2: Platt family break-in, GUILTY. With regard to charge 3: Martin family break-in, GUILTY. With regard to charge 4: Watt family murders, GUILTY OF CAPITAL MURDER. With regard to charge 5: Houston Home break-in, NOT PROVEN. With regard to charge 6: Isabelle Cook murder, GUILTY OF MURDER. With regard to charge 7: Smart family murders, GUILTY OF CAPITAL MURDER. With regard to charge 8: Theft of Smart family car, GUILTY.

Peter Manuel did not agree with the jury's decisions, particularly when they found him guilty of capital murder for the Smart and Watt families. He shook his head in disbelief and was recorded as mumbling obscenities as the foreman read the verdicts. When the dust settled, the jury left the courtroom and Lord Cameron addressed Peter directly. The jury had recommended death by hanging for Peter, and Lord Cameron confirmed his fate. Everyone in the courtroom seemed happy with the verdict, except Peter, who was ushered from the courtroom and moved to a single prisoner holding cell. However, court proceedings were not completely over.

On May 30, 1958, newspapers across the UK and New York featured headlines that read, "Manuel to hang." Residents in the UK, and the friends and families of the victims, were satisfied that law enforcement had apprehended one of the meanest and most gruesome serial killers the country would ever see. Even the pro-life folks who did not support the death penalty were rather quiet given the nature and spectacle of this highly-publicized case.

On June 20, 1958, prison officials, who'd already been watching Peter more closely, fearing he might attempt suicide to avoid hanging, found him "frothing at the mouth" and rushed him to the infirmary. While there, the doctor pumped his stomach and tended to him. No evidence of Peter trying to kill himself was located and he was moved back to his holding cell.

Peter led to his appeal, June 24, 1958.

On June 24, 1958, the appeal that Peter had filed was heard by the Scottish Appellate Court. Essentially, Peter claimed the following errors occurred in his court case:

-The written and verbal confessions he made should not have been admitted as evidence against him,

-He claimed Lord Cameron "misdirected the jury as to the burden of proof" relating to the special defenses,

-The guilty verdict with regard to the

Martin home break-in was "contrary to the evidence:"

-He claimed Lord Cameron misdirected the jury as to the question of motive regarding the Watt family murders,

-He claimed Lord Cameron "failed to summarize the evidence of the witnesses" of Mr. Taylor and Mr. Morrison that fairly supported the special defense of impeachment of Mr. William Watt.

Lastly, he claimed Lord Cameron misdirected the jury "in directing them that the finding of the body and shoe in the Cooke murder could be regarded as independent evidence capable of corroborating the alleged confession."

Peter's appeal was heard in a day but mulled over for over a week by the appellate judge. It's believed the judge spent that time ensuring all of the procedural flaws Peter pointed out were in fact false. He must also take considerable time in considering the appeal while acting fairly and impartially. His ruling, one way or the other, would almost certainly be the final say on whether or not Peter Manuel would remain alive.

At the end of June, Peter Manuel's appeal, on all counts, was denied. The appellate judge found no grounds to dismiss the original findings by Lord Cameron and the jury. All of the claims made by Peter were considered, one by one, and the appellate judge found no weaknesses or deficiencies by Lord Cameron, the jury, or the law enforcement officers and their testimony.

This left Peter with one final desperate effort to save his own life. His struggle to save himself, all of the fear and concern he must have had sensing death was all too close, amounted to a tiny fraction of what he put his victims through. Some said he caught glimpses of the hangman's noose in the prison gallows and it made him crazy.

On July 6, 1958, he filed a Petition for Clemency with Scottish Secretary John McClay. On July 7, 1958, Secretary McClay denied the petition. And so it was done, every card Peter could play, desperately hoping to remain alive, had been played. Finally, after he'd tormented the country for over two years, committing hundreds of crimes, and killing so many people, Peter Manuel would hang for his crimes and meet his own demise.

With every possible way of cheating death for his crimes exhausted, Peter finally came to grips with the fact that he, like his victims, will die.

The United Kingdom hangs Peter Manuel

The last few days Peter had on Earth were not pretty. He was shaved by prison staff (for fear he'd try to cut his own throat with the razor to commit suicide) and watched constantly for fear he'd commit suicide. It seemed the proud and arrogant man who gloated in the courtroom, mocked his victims, and reveled in the fame his trial created, had been physically and emotionally crushed. He no longer acted pompous or feigned confidence while spending most of his last hours in his cell not willing to let others see him. Rightfully so, he was a beaten man.

Prison guards described him as a "shambling mess" and said he rarely spoke to anyone in the prison. In the months during the trial, his celebrity status even inside the prison was grand, but now, with no hope of being saved, Peter had all but given up. While in his cell one night, he tried to act insane (by mumbling, screaming, and bouncing off the walls) and pleaded with the guards that he couldn't have killed anyone because he was not sane. The act and his desperate plea fell on deaf ears. No one felt a shred of remorse for him. Several staff members, prisoners, and law enforcement members could not be happier that Peter would pay for his crimes with his life.

Peter stopped eating and began to pout. He wouldn't let staff dress him and violently kicked at them when they tried to. He did not eat any solid food for almost a week, and it was clear his body was physically breaking down. Medical staff was asked to evaluate him on several occasions, both physically and mentally. At odd hours, he'd request some bread and milk, which he'd gobble up but then later refuse to eat again. His behavior was odd, but not to the point that someone was willing to consider Peter insane.

Over my fifteen-year career, I've seen people deal with death in a hundred different ways. In Peter's case, he'd swallowed his sick criminal pride and didn't quite know how to deal with the fact that he'd be dead soon. I never spoke to the man, but I guarantee he did not consider how the two young teenage girls, the two families, and the taxi-cab driver must have felt when he killed them.

The day before Peter was to be hanged, his parents were allowed to see him. Up until this point, they'd stuck behind him and were convinced that he'd been framed by law enforcement, tricked by the prosecutor, and his rights were violated by Lord Cameron during the trial. However, as Peter spoke with his mother, something came over her, perhaps it was guilt or embarrassment, but she now believed all of the disgusting and terrible things the police said her son had done were in fact true. She was seen slapping Peter in the face while saying, "You can't fool me!" Now, in his darkest hour, even his most vocal supporter, his mother, had seen through his lies and manipulation and was unable to look at her own son.

On July 11, 1958 at approximately 7 a.m., Peter Manuel was scheduled to be awakened to be led to his death. Prison guards found him wide awake, seated in his bed. He was dressed, his hair combed, and he wore a certain look about him as though he'd finally come to understand and appreciate what fate held for him.

Barlinnie Prison Executioner, Harry

Allan, prepared the prison gallows for Peter's execution. He reportedly did not enjoy his job, but it was one he took seriously and he was known for treating the prisoner with a professional attitude. He believed in justice, and in this case, Peter Manuel was accused of several murders, he was found guilty, and he was sentenced to death.

Peter was escorted from the innards of the prison to the gallows, where he finally looked up and saw Mr. Allan and chuckled.

Mr. Allan asked him, "Peter, any last words?"

Peter took in a deep breath and surveyed his surroundings. It had been awhile since fresh air and sunlight had touched his skin. After a few moments he replied, "Turn up the radio, and I'll go quietly."

With that, Mr. Allan placed the hangman's noose around Peter's neck. Reverend Russell Anderson was to Peter's right, quietly saying a small prayer for Peter and his victims.

At approximately 8:01 a.m., Mr. Allan maneuvered the device releasing Peter

Manuel to his death. His feet dangled and he momentarily fought certain death, but his neck broke and he died, as was so ordered, on the gallows. Those around the prison that day suggest Peter might have finally been put at ease when life left his body; others said good riddance and hoped never to see someone so terrible as Peter Manuel again.

A few moments later, Peter Manuel, the United Kingdom's "Beast of Birkenshaw," was lowered to the ground, the noose removed, and his lifeless body placed in a wooden cart. Mr. Allan pushed the cart and Peter's body across the Barlinnie Prison gallows to an area where a grave had been dug. With the help of another prison staff member, Peter's body was lowered into the grave, he was covered in dirt, and the deed was finally complete. His grave was left unmarked and has not been disturbed since.

Peter Manuel's Case Draws Scrutiny

Two weeks after Peter was dead and buried, local officials focused on several unsolved murders in the United Kingdom. One cold case that spurred their interest was the murder of Sydney Dunn. There had been enormous speculation by locals and the police that Peter had killed Sydney, but not much evidence had been collected at the time that tied him to the killing.

Police revealed that their records confirmed Peter was in Newcastle upon Tyne, Northumberland, England, the area where Mr. Dunn was found, at the same time the murder occurred. Northumberland Police noted that Peter was in the town looking for employment. In fact, it was noted that Peter admitted to attending a job interview in the area where Mr. Dunn was murdered.

The investigation also revealed that a search of Mr. Dunn's taxi led to police locating a jacket button on the floorboard, a button they said came from Peter's jacket. His clothing had been booked as evidence when he was arrested originally while possessing Mr. Smart's banknotes. The jacket they collected had a button missing, and the button they found in Mr. Dunn's vehicle matched the remaining buttons on the jacket.

As a result, Peter Manuel was tried posthumously for the murder of Sydney Dunn. Based on the new evidence, although fairly weak and circumstantial, Peter was found guilty of Sydney Dunn's murder. For that time period, this was an interesting turn of events as not many people had been tried for cases, especially murder, once the suspect was dead. If anything, it provided some small bit of closure for Mr. Dunn's family that in a way, justice had been served for his murder and Peter paid the ultimate price because of it.

*****

On Wednesday, April 30, 2008, BBC News printed a story that shook the community regarding the serial killings committed by Peter Manuel. An attorney, Dr. Richard Goldberg of Aberdeen University's Law School, publicly declared that "vital information" in Peter's court trial was purposely suppressed "to ensure Peter was hanged."

Dr. Goldberg claimed his father observed a medical examination of Peter Manuel while working as a consultant at the Western Infirmary in Glasgow. Dr. Goldberg said Peter's life may have been spared had the court known "the full extent of his (Peter's) health problems, which included a form of epilepsy many believe can cause criminal behavior."

He went on to say that "the possibility of Manuel having a mental disorder might have led to a diminished responsibility verdict rather than execution."

Dr. Goldberg added: "I think there was considerable evidence that he was a psychopath, there was debate over whether there should be a reprieve, and in my view insufficient weight was given to that evidence and also to the fact that Manuel suffered from temporal lobe epilepsy."

Attempting to further his view he stated, "To me, it is in the public interest that we have access to this information, that the public should see that justice was done properly, and they should have access to everything in the Manuel files."

The article points out that more than fifty years after the highly publicized trial have passed and there are still certain files in various courts that are closed. Back in 2008, he advised that it was near impossible to locate or gain access to all of the files pertaining to Peter Manuel's trial. I can attest to his concern and the difficult task he endured. I too spent months making phone calls, sending letters, and emails looking for similar data. Unlike Dr. Goldberg, I do not think the effort required was a direct result of anyone trying to cover up the past.

The article noted, as did I, that significant efforts were made by the Scottish Home Department to convict Peter Manuel for the murders. His contention was that the Scottish Home Department did not think Peter was a psychopath. He felt they would have said even if he was a psychopath, he was marginally one at best, so he should have still been hanged for his crimes.

According to Dr. Goldberg, "The problem is that psychopathic personality disorder still is not a basis for a plea of diminished responsibility, unlike in England, and this remains an anomaly."

Interestingly enough, the High Court ordered in 1958 that a portion of the trial data be sealed for seventy-five years. It's unclear why the ruling was made, but at the time no one considered it a red flag because law enforcement had apprehended a serial killer and he would later be found guilty and sentenced to death.

Russell Galbraith, a journalist covering Peter's trial, noted little opposition to executing Peter. He explained that even anti-capital punishment protestors were quiet for the most part.

Galbraith said, "I don't remember any great enthusiasm from people trying to save Manuel, I must say, although there was obviously an abhorrence at the death penalty in many places."

Mr. Galbraith's position with regard to Peter Manuel's involvement in the murders he was convicted of, and whether or not he was sane or insane when committing the murders, is interesting but lacks foundation. Numerous psychiatric evaluations were performed on Peter Manuel throughout his many years of criminal behavior and time he spent in custody in prisons, jail, and the borstal. The reports (admittedly not all of them) are available to read and form your own opinion. None of the psychologists or psychiatrists who prepared reports that I read while preparing to write this book noted any indication that Peter was insane.

The fact the Crown sealed a large portion of Peter's case for a period of seventy-five years, which was not a normal practice (especially for such a long period of time), does allow conspiracy theorists some foundation; however, without knowing the facts (contained in the sealed documents) I choose not to speculate on whether or not the Crown had any involvement with a cover-up against Peter Manuel.

To be fair, Mr. Galbraith also noted that if it was proven in court that Peter was insane or suffered from a mental health issue, he may have been spared receiving the death penalty. I don't know if that is true. We can only speculate as to what Peter's fate would have been had it been proven in court that Peter suffered mentally and, because of his mental health issues, he killed nine people over a two-year period. However, after researching this case for six months and reading thousands of pages of newspaper articles, court minutes, court documents, police reports, archived files, confession letters from Peter, and any other piece of information I could collect, I truly believe Peter would have still received the death penalty for his crimes.

*****

In 2009, notable United Kingdom solicitor Allan Nicol argued quite well his position concerning a little known fact about Peter Manuel - the fact that he (Peter) had a secret sexual disorder. Nicol, based on his research, strongly believed that Peter was unable to be satisfied by "normal sexual activity" and "suffered from paraphilia." Paraphilia, according to various acceptable scholarly definitions, is the need for abnormal stimulus to sexual arousal or orgasm.

Mr. Nicol has said that Peter was an "inadequate sexual psychopath who took pleasure from the control he had over people before he killed them."

As noted earlier in this book, Peter was charged with rape and convicted of the charge in 1946. Mr. Nicol alleges the charge and conviction of rape should not have occurred because physical and psychological reasons would have made it impossible for Peter to achieve an erection and, therefore, he'd be unable to rape his victim.

"The clear implication is that he achieved sexual relief through violence and required a stronger stimulus after each attack. He achieved his satisfaction in other ways," Mr. Nicol said of the case. He pointed out that the victim told police she was raped and evidence suggested (her pants were down and there was bruising on her body) that she'd been raped. However, Mr. Nicol also pointed out that the victim was "dazed after being battered by Manuel" and no medical evidence had been gathered (such as sexual injury or semen) by the police when they charged Peter with rape.

Mr. Nicol requested a second forensic specialist examine Peter's clothing from the night of the alleged rape. He explained that the second investigation of the clothing revealed, "complete sperm were found on his trousers, shirt, and singlet. But, his dark secret meant he did not actually commit the full crime. He would have raped had he been capable, but he was not capable."

Recall when Peter attacked Mary

McLaughlan. Mr. Nicol believes Peter actually "lay with her for more than an hour as locals and policemen prowled (while looking for both of them)." Mr. Nicol offered, "She wasn't to know the necessary excitement process for Manuel to achieve satisfaction had begun with them lying together." Mr. Nicol believes Peter had "outlined her (Mary's) fate. Her head was to be severed and buried. He (Peter) groped and forced kisses on her."

"His eyes bulged and contorted in pleasure as he growled. She sobbed and pleaded. Suddenly, he stopped. He stopped groping and sat back."

"She had escaped rape. She was about to become the last of Manuel's victims of violence who would be allowed to live to testify."

Mr. Nicol spoke about the Smart and Watt murders. He explained, "The absence of semen is regarded as significant in that the perpetrator either fulfilled his goal spontaneously at the crime scene or later with the aid of mementoes from the victim." It is Mr. Nicol's belief that Peter took items from the homes after killing the victims that he would later use to help him achieve an ejaculation.

Lastly, in a point I completely agree with, Mr. Nicol believed had Peter remained out of custody, the need to kill again would have come again and he would have killed continuously until removed from the public.

*****

In 2010, a cold case for the murder of Mary "Molly" Terris was re-opened. She was killed at a mine near Falkirk in 1949, but the case had no leads and remained shelved as a "cold case" for almost sixty years. Law enforcement received a new lead in her murder from the records maintained by a former detective inspector that investigated her murder.

The inspector believes Charles Tallis, a career criminal and friend of Peter Manuel, killed Mary Terris. According to his records, Charles Tallis allegedly confessed to Peter Manuel that he killed Ms. Terris while the two of them were housed at Peterhead Prison.

According to the inspector, he believes Tallis's confession about killing Ms. Terris, thirty-one years old at the time, inspired

Peter to begin his own killing spree. The evidence the inspector says he has, although only circumstantial, is enough to conclude that Charles Tallis was the killer.

Oddly enough, the officer refused to identify himself and was quoted as saying, "Despite an extensive police inquiry at the time of Molly Terris's murder, no strong suspects were identified, no direct positive lines of inquiry were raised and the trail went cold." He added, "Papers relating to the inquiry were placed in storage where they remained untouched until now.

"After seven months of investigative work I believe I have uncovered several compelling circumstantial factors linking Tallis to the murder."

The inspector noted that Charles Tallis died in 1977, at the age of 65.

He said he brought forward his suspicion hoping that someone in the community "might remember some information or a pub conversation they had with him (Tallis) that would assist the police in this case."

One of the main things the inspector

points to as connecting Tallis to the murder is the fact that Tallis worked in a mine before his criminal career began. The inspector believes Tallis would have been able to use his knowledge to break into and enter into the office of the mine and get inside the safe after killing Ms. Terris. Based on the new information provided by the anonymous inspector, the Central Scotland Police confirmed that they were considering the new information and re-opening the cold murder case. This was newsworthy because Peter Manuel had been considered the main suspect in this murder.

A representative from the Central Scotland Police unit stated, "We would be interested in any information that resulted in the person or persons responsible for the death of Molly Terris in 1949 being traced."

"We are considering information which has been collated by a former officer of Central Scotland Police."

The case remains open, but unsolved.

From time to time, articles related to Peter Manuel will surface. Although his case has been investigated and discussed for a very long time, new information, some of which is highly contested, comes out causing further discussion about such a massive case. Since Peter was hanged, many cold cases throughout the United Kingdom have been closely examined to see if Peter had any involvement in the case. Police will continue to investigate any leads that may surface in the hopes of closing cases, specifically any murder or missing person cases committed during the time Peter Manuel walked on earth.

It appears the entire Peter Manuel case, including *all* case files, court files, and court minutes, may be opened or accessible in 2033. The Crown sealed several documents for a period of 75 years in 1958 when the case was adjudicated. Many people will be interested in the contents of this data, but it's likely nothing that would have changed the course of Peter Manuel or one's opinion about the man. If anything, revealing these files may likely open old wounds and spawn a useless debate about what could have or should have been done by all the people involved in the case. None of it will matter since Peter was hanged and the cases (that he was known to be involved in) were closed. As an investigator and member of law enforcement, I'm hopeful the release of such data might help solve more crimes committed by Peter Manuel.

The Psychology of a Serial Killer

Beyond Dr. Galbraith, there are others (the number grows almost daily) who are still divided regarding Peter Manuel's mental state when he killed nine people. It's been noted quite often that he displayed many classic traits of a psychopath: he lacked empathy for his victims, he showed no remorse for killing them, later denied doing so, and never accepted that his behavior was unacceptable and wrong. Still, some doctors who interviewed or evaluated Peter noted specifically that he suffered memory loss, epilepsy, and had fugue states. Fugue state is a rare psychiatric disorder characterized by reversible amnesia for personal identity, including the memories, personality, and other identifying characteristics of individuality. It's been said several times that epilepsy could have driven Peter to kill, but this idea was never fully investigated or understood.

However, when we try to grasp who Peter was, several contradictions come to mind: He killed and raped women yet loved his mother fiercely and unconditionally; he was known to kick and maim animals as a child, but absolutely adored the family dog; he could never keep a relationship with women, but he considered himself as a "player" or "gigolo."

Many years later, some familiar with Peter's case diagnosed him with Psychopathic Personality Disorder (PPD). It was not a well-known term or concept in 1958, but based on what we know about the disorder now, and what facts are available in this case, it appears, at least in part, that Peter Manuel did have Psychopathic Personality Disorder. However, even in an extreme form, this diagnosis would never make anything he did acceptable. I refuse to rationalize a serial killer's inner demons as reason to murder innocent victims time and time again.

Psychopathic Personality Disorder has been closely associated to sociopathy, a much larger and more broad scope of the human mind and behavior. Three main categories describe a subject who experiences the disorder and sheds light as to why a person behaves a certain way. Primarily, Peter Manuel was described as displaying antisocial behavior, disinhibited and bold actions, and he clearly had diminished remorse and empathy for what he'd done. As these psychological factors migrated around and through Peter's mind, they influenced his actions.

With regard to Peter's boldness, consider the Smart family murders. He broke into their home, found them asleep, and killed them without remorse. He then stayed in their home for almost a week, clinically displaying low fear and a high toleration of danger and unfamiliarity. Peter's confidence was at an all-time high when he temporarily took over the Smart home.

With regard to Peter's disinhibition, consider Peter's plan to sexually assault and not murder (at least according to his own statements) Isabelle or Anne, and how things went brutally wrong in the blink of an eye. He later told a psychologist that he acted most of the time based on his impulses and had no real plans when he saw the girls for the first time. He also said he never planned to kill the two families he murdered, but rather only meant to burglarize their homes. However, Peter could not control himself once he got going; nothing in his head rang loudly to tell him to stop or remind him that his actions were unacceptable, inhumane, and never should have happened. Likewise, Peter's insatiable demand for immediate gratification and the inability to restrain himself complements the classic definition of disinhibition for someone diagnosed with Psychopathic Personality Disorder.

Within PPD is another concept identified as "meanness." The most accepted definition for meanness would be "lacking empathy and close attachments with others, disdain of close attachments, use of cruelty to gain empowerment, exploitative tendencies, defiance of authority, and destructive excitement seeking." After reading this book, you should have numerous examples of Peter Manuel being mean and downright dirty. In fact, Peter was mean to everyone and every animal he encountered, except his own family and the family dog.

I often hear questions such as this: How does psychopathy affect one's aptitude to become a criminal? Specifically, researchers often discuss three main points: Criminality, violence, and sexual offending. Researchers tend to agree that a correlation between psychopathy and crime exists;

however, there are cases on both sides of the coin indicating we still don't know for sure the entire role psychopathy plays in people committing crime, at least not definitively.

With regard to criminality, studies within North America and abroad have concluded that one's psychopathy is affected by disciplinary infractions, repeated imprisonment, substance misuse, and detention in higher security. Peter checked most of these concepts off the list; however, it's unclear if he abused drugs.

With regard to violence, psychopathy has been associated with an increased risk of violence, but too many conflicting studies exist to be entirely sure how they correlate. Still, a large percentage (70%-93% depending on who crunches the numbers) of people who have committed murder have also been diagnosed with some sort of psychological component or disorder. In the United States, several reports released by the Federal Bureau of Investigation (FBI) clearly indicate that "psychopathic behavior is consistent with traits common to some serial killers, including sensation seeking, a lack of remorse or guilt, impulsivity, the need for control, and predatory behavior."

With regard to sexual offending, specifically child molesters, psychopathy is associated to this crime set. Some studies I've examined indicated that criminal psychopaths prefer violent sexual behavior. Statistics, at least within the United States and Canada, support this claim. Aggression in sexual murderers is also quite high with psychopaths, including sadistic violence. Peter Manuel clearly demonstrated levels of PPD and general psychopathic tendencies while on his criminal and murderous two-year spree before finally being apprehended.

Being short in stature and having the thick American accent (when he was younger because it eventually went away and was replaced with a Scottish accent) made him a target as a child. Being the butt of jokes, having kids finger pointing at him daily, and having to fight kids all the time certainly hurt Peter in the beginning. The same things also made Peter mean when he grew up. He'd eventually turn the tables on everyone and become more mean than one would think possible.

We've discussed Peter's heavy American accent and how children from the UK teased him daily about his accent and his short stature. It's fair to say he was bullied and, as a result, Peter sought a way to escape his anger and frustration from being picked on. There have been several documented cases throughout the world where kids being bullied have become murderers.

Peter started with breaking and entering before committing murder. The rush and excitement while doing so covered the sadness he felt from not being accepted in his new surroundings. In addition, his family did not have much money, and Peter stole items to pawn them to buy things he wanted. At some point, the same kids who teased him began to see the nice things he had and became at least inwardly jealous.

Peter as a teenager learned to fight (based on the fact he was short and kids challenged him often and as a means to release his anger), enjoyed being the center of attention, and began hanging out with kids of similar ilk. His parents did nothing to curb his behavior; in fact, they would lie to police several times in an effort to protect him. They left a wounded child to fend for himself and never gave him the "tough love" he needed to correct his life path. With no one to guide him, Peter graduated from breaking and entering to assaults and eventually murder.

I personally believe wires in his head were certainly crossed at birth. Many psychological and sociological factors contributed to Peter Manuel becoming a serial killer, but I'm not entirely convinced he was born relatively normal. I've known many criminals with backgrounds similar to Peter who did not commit crimes their entire lives. Many found the courage and guidance to get out of the gutter and make something of their lives. None of them became a serial killer.

Peter was forced into a Borstal (ordered to the prison for kids because he'd committed so many crimes) based on his progressively worse behavior and was a teenager when he entered one. He lived with other boys with serious criminal and mental health issues that society had no answer for. What came of it, similar to the American prison system, is a person being released armed with greater skills to commit more crimes. It's a reciprocal system in which those inside rarely rise above. Peter not only failed to rise above his situation, he fell so far to the bottom that he became a selfish murderer. By no means do I blame anyone but Peter for his behavior, but refusing to acknowledge his poor socialization and lack of support as at least marginally contributing to his behavior would do my research an injustice.

Specifically disturbing for me with regard to Peter's behavior was the fact that he murdered the Smart family in cold blood, then remained in their home, eating their food, drinking their drinks, and feeding their cat. He broke into their home, systematically killed them, and then hung out for a week as if what he'd done meant absolutely nothing to him. How could it not register in his head that what he'd done was so wrong? It was as though he was mocking the victims by remaining in their home and later stealing items, including banknotes, which later led to him being apprehended.

I shudder considering how many more people Peter would have killed had he not gotten sloppy. Hanging out at bars and buying drinks with banknotes from a family he murdered infuriates me. He was so reckless, so brazen, and acting as though he was untouchable. He lived three steps ahead of the police and enjoyed toying with them. Going as far as giving an inspector a ride to look for Isabelle Cooke, a young girl he murdered, and telling the inspector they were looking in the wrong place for her body, indicates just how cocky and twisted Peter had become.

Unlike some serial killers, there does not appear to be one single event that sparked the homicidal rage Peter exhibited. He had a girlfriend, Anne O'Hara, for a small period of time as an adult, but they called off their brief engagement rather quickly. She cited religious differences, and Peter told everyone he didn't even care for Ms. O'Hara. Obviously the break-up bothered him, but it's unclear how much (or if at all) it contributed to his behavior and decisions. Recall that two of his victims were young girls that Peter dominated then killed. Although Peter never discussed his motives for killing, it appears the turbulent relationship with Ms. O'Hara may have sparked at least some of his fury.

Peter Anthony Manuel was one of if not the worst serial killer the United Kingdom had ever seen. His crimes and the highly-publicized trial captivated people around the globe. The fact Peter represented himself (for the majority of the main trial), and at times did a decent job while doing so, confused people. How could someone so articulate commit such heinous crimes? How could he present as a clean-cut and thoughtful person in court, yet be responsible for so many deaths? Peter reveled in the attention and had above average intelligence. He'd spent a considerable amount of time in courts around the United Kingdom and in custody. During that time, he learned the language and procedures used in court, so when his time came – to take the ultimate stage - he excelled and lived in the moment. However, he could not maintain the charade and was severely crushed by the officers, prosecutor, and the judge.

In the end, it was Peter's cockiness and arrogance that led to him being apprehended by the police. He truly felt he was more intelligent and more cunning than every police officer in the United Kingdom. The same arrogance and cocky attitude, the one he loved to display for the cameras and the media, also led to him being found guilty during his trial.

Had he allowed Mr. Leslie to represent him throughout the proceedings and stayed off the stand, there is a small chance Peter would have not been hanged for his crimes.

There's no doubt in my mind that Peter would have been found guilty of the murders regardless of who represented him, but a sound attorney may have been able to introduce the psychological aspects Peter had. Entering into the case the fact Peter had psychological issues might have spared his life.

Ultimately, the same cockiness and arrogance that Peter used when killing his victims led to his death, a fitting conclusion for the families and friends of the victims and those in the community who lived in fear until "The Beast of Birkenshaw" was hanged on the gallows. Mr. Allan confirmed the monster was finally dead, and a period of peace followed...until the next serial killer struck.

Acknowledgments

As many of you know, complex serial killer investigations can consume a person. A whole agency can crumble and be pushed to the brink of cracking under the immense pressure of bringing closure to grieving families, satisfying the public's demand for answers, and capturing or eliminating the killer. After the fact, sometimes many decades later, securing the minute details of what a serial killer did, why they did it, and what might have led to them becoming a monster is challenging. As such, I'd like to thank the following people, associations, and groups for assisting me with the collection of data for this book. My work relies on the supreme efforts of others, and I appreciate each of you immensely. For the men and women in law enforcement, stay frosty and safe. And to all of you, take care and hug your family and friends every chance you get.

Law Enforcement
Lanarkshire Police
Glasgow Police

West Midlands Police
Northumberland Police
Constable Robert Smith
Gordon Gillies, Advocate Depute, lead prosecutor on the Peter Manuel case.
Superintendent Hendry, Lanarkshire CID
Glasgow High Court, Justice Cameron
Sheriff Allan Walker
Scottish Secretary, John McClay
Det. Superintendent Alexander Brown, Lanarkshire Police
Inspector Matthew Cleland, Lanarkshire Police
Det. Inspector Robert McNeil, Lanarkshire Police, primary inspector for the Smart family murders.
Harry Allan, prison executioner.

Acquaintances
Anne O'Hara (engaged to her, but never marries).
Dr. Anderson, interviewed Peter Manuel at Barlinnie Prison.
Harald Leslie, original attorney for Peter (Peter fired him nine days into the trial).
Peter Hamilton
Tony Lowe, possessed the Beretta firearm

Peter used to kill the Smart family.

Ferguson Rodger, Professor who interviewed Peter.

Dandy McKay, known criminal and friend of Peter's.

Peter said he gave him the Smart family banknotes.

Charles Tallis, known criminal friend of Peter's. Peter said he gave him an electric razor which was later proven to be taken from the Smart home.

Research

Lanarkshire Police reports.
Glasgow Police reports.
Scotland Court Archived Files
Manchester Court Archived File
Beverly Court Archived File
Yorkshire Court Archived Files
National Archives of Scotland
Department of Psychology, Radford University
Scottish Daily Press
BBC News (hardcopy newspapers).
BBC News (online).
BBC Programme, *Inside the Mind of a Psychopath.*

Crime and Investigation (CI), United Kingdom.
The Daily Record, United Kingdom.
TruTV Crime Library
Wikipedia.com
Murderpedia.com
Crimelibrary.com

The Victims
Anne Kneilands, 17
Marion Watt, 45
Vivienne Watt (Marion's daughter), 17
Margaret Brown, 41
Sydney Dunn, 36
Isabelle Cooke, 17
Peter Smart, 45
Doris Smart (Peter's wife), 42
Michael Smart (Peter and Doris's son), 10
Mary McLaughlan, attacked by Peter, but survived.

About the Author

Chris Swinney is a Police Officer in the San Francisco Bay area. His writing includes the bestselling '_Bill Dix Detective Series_' which are fiction books based on his experience as a cop.

Swinney has also written four bestselling true crime books:

Robert Pickton: The Pig Farmer Killer

The Killer Handyman: The True Story of William Patrick Fyfe

Robert Black: The True Story of a Child Rapist and Serial Killer from the UK

Deadly Voices: The True Story of Serial Killer Herbert Mullin

Chris is a big time supporter of Teachers, Parents, Law Enforcement, Doctors, Nurses, Firefighters, American Troops, Juvenile Diabetes Research, and children. He spends time volunteering for his church, at schools, he coaches, and every once in awhile he gets to go fly fishing.

Visit Chris's Publisher's Page:
rjparkerpublishing.com/c-l--swinney.html

Amazon's Author Page:
http://amzn.to/1LukWVr

Made in the USA
Middletown, DE
13 May 2018